D1325794

LATIN MATTERS

Also available in the series:
Shakespeare Matters

First published in the United Kingdom in 2008 by
Portico Books
10 Southcombe Street
London
W14 0RA

An imprint of Anova Books Company Ltd

ISBN 9781906032319

A CIP catalogue record for this book is available from the British Library.

10 9 8 7 6 5 4 3 2 1

Reproduction by Rival Colour Ltd., UK
Printed and bound by CT Printing Ltd., China

This book can be ordered direct from the publisher.
Contact the marketing department, but try your bookshop first.

www.anovabooks.com

LATIN MATTERS

SIMON R.H. JAMES

ipsa scientia potestas est
(Sir Francis Bacon, 1597)

PORTICO

LATIN MATTERS

INTRODUCTION

Latin trains the brain. End of story. That is the short response.

As a Latin schoolmaster, I frequently come across challenges of my subject as 'boring' (in other words difficult), 'irrelevant', and 'dead' … and it isn't always just from the pupils. But good sport these challenges provide. Though these mischievous inquiries from my youthful charges are often without sound mind and judgement (they think 'dead' is a real wind-up), others are indeed genuine and require a respectful reply.

Poor old Latin: it comes under assault from all kinds of *non cognoscenti* who claim its anachronistic tendencies as an easy target in these dark days of dumbing down.

Well, you've read this far so you should be interested in sharing some of my ammunition to add rigour in our defence against any force that would undermine clear thought and spoil the fun.

Latin is difficult.

But more so is passing through the eye of a needle. The harder something is, the greater the challenge. Give it a go. That rare 'click' of a breakthrough, where once was darkness, is revelatory. And once the light shines, one wonders what there was to fear.

Latin is supremely relevant: it's survived for 2,500 years, which is an amazing feat by any measure you could deem worthy. Dominant during the Roman Empire, kept alive by the Church in the Dark Ages and then revitalised by the Renaissance and the invention of printing, Latin deserves more attention than it presently receives. It's omnipresent in archaeology, history, geography, geology, physics, chemistry, biology, botany, astronomy, art, law, religion, literature, music, language, technology and mathematics. Life is less confusing with a little Latin. And I've found it much clearer with a lot of Latin. The coming pages should illustrate this claim beyond question.

And as for claims to the language being 'dead'? Well, the answer is yes and no.

Mostly no.

The language now known as Latin and studied in

textbooks is the formal written version so it has never been spoken. Except now that it is – since English has taken words such as *post mortem, agenda, arena, exit, vertigo, et cetera* and thousands of others as its own with a modern spin. The spoken version, commonly known as 'Vulgar Latin', is the one that has evolved and would have been far removed from the written stuff. Language, once spoken, enjoys flexibility in grammar, vocabulary and accent. Eventually it is liable to split itself into regional dialects. It is unlikely that a Gallic Roman would have ever understood a Turkish Roman, but, as with the standardised Chinese Mandarin of today, they could read the same newspaper.

In fact spoken remnants of Latin even exist now in the odd Swiss canton, central Sardinia and in Vatican City where it is the official language, while Mass is conducted in ecclesiastical Latin. The Romantic languages French, Spanish, Portuguese, Romanian and Italian emerged from the Vulgar Latin. Needless to say the study of Latin is a considerable help when learning these languages, but since at least 60 per cent of English is derived from Latin it is very useful here too.

Latin has proved an exceptional *lingua franca*. Until

recently all documents and treatises were written in Latin thus crossing all international borders without risking any offence between one nation to another. Now English, another successful linguistic story, has that role.

And why keep Latin in schools? Its cultural output stands proudly alongside nations past and present. It has a wonderfully consistent grammar. And knowing one grammar thoroughly helps to build up and learn other languages. Grammar offers precision, clarity of thought, fluidity and comprehension. There should be no shame in trying to express oneself as clearly and as succinctly as possible. Loss of language risks anarchy and a lack of communication provokes a life without rules.

Latin's logic and structure truly demands discipline and triggers thought, and young minds feed voraciously on clear answers rather than the grey areas. Show school children the finishing line and make it challenging enough to reach and they will respond and beat all expectation.

In short it trains the brain.

HARRY POTTER

It's well known that Joanne K. Rowling studied French and Classics at Exeter University, and it seems she put some of her time there to good use – which is not how I remember university. Many of the spells, charms, curses and hexes incanted in the amazingly successful *Harry Potter* septilogy / heptalogy are a mixture of Latin and Greek without paying too much attention to grammar. The Hogwart's motto *draco dormiens nunquam titillandus* (a sleeping dragon should never be tickled), in particular, attractively contains both a participle and gerundive of obligation and is as fine a motto as any inspiring wizard would need to get through the day.

The following incantations are observed in some or all of Rowling's seven epics;

1. Philosopher's Stone
2. Chamber of Secrets
3. Prisoner Of Azkaban

Incantation if known	Book	Derivation	Effect
ACCIO	4,6,7	*accio* (I SUMMON)	SUMMONING CHARM
AGUAMENTI	6,7	*aqua* (WATER), *mens* (MIND)	ISSUES WATER FROM A WAND
ALOHOMORA	1	*mora* (DELAY) *with Hawaiian for goodbye*	UNLOCKS DOORS
APARECIUM	2	*appareo* (I APPEAR)	REVEALS INVISIBLE INKS
AVIS	4,6	*avis* (BIRD)	ISSUES BIRDS FROM A WAND
CAVE INIMICUM	7	*caveo* (I BEWARE), *inimicus* (ENEMY)	STRENGTHENS CAMP'S DEFENCES
COLLOPORTUS	5	*colligo* (I BIND), *porta* (DOOR)	LOCKS DOORS
CONFRINGO	7	*confringo* (I SHATTER)	EXPLODES OBJECTS
CONFUNDO	3,4,6	*confundo* (I CONFOUND)	CAUSES PERPLEXITY
CONJUNCTIVITIS CURSE	4,5	*coniunctiva* (of the eye)	DAMAGES EYESIGHT
CRUCIO	4	*crucio* (I TORMENT)	CAUSES EXTREME PAIN *(one of the 3 unforgivable curses)*
DEFODIO	7	*defodio* (I DIG OUT)	DIGS A WAY OUT
DELETRIUS	4	*deleo* (I DESTROY)	DEFENCE AGAINST *prior incantato*
DENSAUGEO	4	*dens* (TOOTH), *augeo* (I INCREASE)	CAUSES TEETH TO GROW
DESCENDO	7	*descendo* (I DESCEND)	LOWERS OBJECTS

Incantation if known	Book	Derivation	Effect
DIFFINDO	4,6,7	*diffundo* (I SCATTER)	SPLITS AN OBJECT
DISSENDIUM	3	*dissimulo* (I DISGUISE)	OPENS A STATUE'S HUMP FOR SECRET PATH TO HOGSMEADE
DURO	7	*duro* (I HARDEN)	TURNS TARGET TO STONE
ERECTO	7	*erigo* (I BUILD)	ERECTS A TENT
EVANESCO	5	*evanesco* (I VANISH)	CAUSES DISAPPEARANCE
EXPECTO PATRONUM	3–7	*expecto* (I AWAIT), *patronus* (PATRON)	SUMMONS A PERSONAL GUARDIAN TO WARD OFF DEMENTORS
EXPELLIARMUS	2–7	*expello* (I EXPEL), *arma* (WEAPONS)	DISARMS OPPONENT
FIDELIUS CHARM	3,5,7	*fidelis* (TRUSTWORTHY)	ENTRUSTS A SECRET TO A KEEPER
FINITE (INCANTATEM)	2,5,7	*finio* (I END), *incantatio* (SPELL)	BREAKS SPELLS
FLAGRATE	5	*flagro* (I BURN)	SUMMONS FIRE
FURNUNCULUS	4	*furunculus* (A BOIL)	BRINGS OUT BOILS ON A VICTIM
GEMINIO	7	*geminus* (TWIN)	DUPLICATES OBJECTS
HOMINEM REVELIO	7	*homo* (MAN), *revelo* (I REVEAL)	REVEALS HUMANS
HOMORPHUS CURSE	2	*homo* (MAN) WITH GREEK FOR CHANGE	USED TO CHANGE A WEREWOLF INTO A MAN OR VICE VERSA
IMPEDIMENTA	4	*impedimentum* (HINDRANCE)	CREATES HURDLES FOR ATTACKERS
IMPERIO	4,7	*imperium* (COMMAND)	CONTROLS VICTIM'S ACTIONS
IMPERVIUS	3,5,7	*impervius* (IMPASSABLE)	REPELS SUBSTANCES
INANIMATUS CONIURUS	5	*inanimus* (INANIMATE), *coniuro* (I PLOT)	POSSIBLY CONJURES INANIMATE OBJECTS
INCARCEROUS	5,6	*carcer* (PRISON)	TRAPS WITH ROPES
INCENDIO	1,4,6	*incendium* (FIRE)	STARTS A FIRE

Incantation if known	Book	Derivation	Effect
LEGILIMENS	5,6	lego (I READ), mens (MIND)	READS MINDS
LEVICORPUS	5,6,7	levo (I LIFT), corpus (BODY)	DANGLES VICTIM UPSIDE DOWN
LIBERACORPUS	6	libero (I FREE), corpus (BODY)	FREES ONE FROM levicorpus
LOCOMOTOR	5,7	locus (PLACE), moveo (I MOVE)	LEVITATES AN OBJECT
LOCOMOTOR MORTIS	1,6	AS ABOVE, mors (DEATH)	RENDERS IMMOBILE
LUMOS	2–7	lumen (LIGHT)	LIGHTS END OF WAND
MOBILIARBUS	3	mobilis (MOBILE), arbor (TREE)	LEVITATES A TREE
MOBILICORPUS	3	mobilis (MOBILE), corpus (BODY)	LEVITATES A BODY
MORSMORDRE	4,6	mors (DEATH), mordeo (I BITE)	CREATES THE DARK MARK
NOX	3,7	nox (NIGHT)	PUTS OUT LIGHT AT END OF WAND
OBLIVIATE	2,7	obliviscor (I FORGET)	CAUSES MEMORY LOSS
OPPUGNO	6	oppugno (I ATTACK)	CONJURES CREATURES TO ATTACK A TARGET
PETRIFICUS TOTALUS	1–7	petra (ROCK), totus (WHOLE)	CAUSES VICTIM'S LOSS OF MOBILITY
PORTUS	5	porta (GATE)	TURNS OBJECT INTO PORTKEY
PRIORI INCANTATEM	4	prior (FORMER), incantatio (SPELL)	REVEALS WAND'S PREVIOUS SPELL
PROTEGO	4–7	protego (I PROTECT)	PROVIDES A SHIELD AGAINST SPELL
PROTEGO HORRIBILIS	7	protego (I PROTECT), horribilis (HORRIBLE)	PROTECTS AGAINST DARK MAGIC

LATIN MATTERS

Incantation if known	Book	Derivation	Effect
PROTEGO TOTALUM	7	*protego* (I PROTECT), *totus* (WHOLE)	PROTECTS AN AREA
QUIETUS	4	*quietus* (QUIET)	SOFTENS A VICTIM'S VOICE
REDUCIO	4	*reduco* (I LEAD BACK)	REDUCES SOLID OBJECTS
REDUCTO	4,5,6	*reduco* (I LEAD BACK)	DESTROYS OBJECTS
RENNERVATE	4,6	*nervus* (STRENGTH)	BRINGS CONSCIOUSNESS
REPARO	4–7	*reparo* (I RENEW)	FIXES BROKEN OBJECTS
REPELLO MUGGLETUM	7	*repello* (I REPEL)	KEEPS PESKY MUGGLES AWAY
RICTUSEMPRA	2	*rideo* (I LAUGH), *semper* (ALWAYS)	INDUCES LAUGHTER
RIDDIKULUS	3,4,5	*ridiculus* (LAUGHABLE)	TURNS A BOGGART INTO FIGURE OF FUN
SALVIO HEXIA	7	*salvo* (I SAVE)	STRENGTHENS AN AREA
SECTUMSEMPRA	6,7	*seco* (I CUT), *semper* (ALWAYS)	SLASHES VICTIM
SERPENSORTIA	2	*serpens* (SNAKE)	SNAKE APPEARS FROM WAND
SILENCIO	5	*silentium* (SILENCE)	SILENCES VICTIM
SONORUS	4,7	*sono* (I MAKE A NOISE)	AMPLIFIES A VOICE
SPECIALIS REVELIO	6	*specialis* (SPECIFIC), *revelo* (I REVEAL)	UNVEILS INGREDIENTS OF POTION
TERGEO	6,7	*tergeo* (I WIPE)	CLEANS UP
WINGARDIUM LEVIOSA	1,7	*levo* (I LIFT)	CAUSES LEVITATION

A little bit of latin...

Great stories but probably and sadly apocryphal

Sir Francis Drake started the ball rolling upon witnessing the flight of the Spanish Armada and is reputed to have quipped *'Cantharides'* – the medical name for the aphrodisiac known as, wait for it, the Spanish fly.

Upon capturing Sind in 1843 General Sir Charles Napier, he of the statue in Trafalgar Square, sent a one-word dispatch to the Foreign Office, Governor General or his brother, depending on the version one reads, *'peccavi'* – I have sinned. It is accepted that a Punch cartoon first started this story. Similarly in 1857 Lieutenant General Sir Colin Campbell or Lord Clyde captured Lucknow during the Indian Mutiny and was credited with the telegram *'nunc fortunatus sum'* – I am in luck now.

Lord Dalhousie annexed Oudh in 1856 with the dubious dispatch *'vovi'* – I have vowed.

THE BEATLES

In 1995 Dr Jukka Ammondt, a Finnish teacher, gained praise for translating, performing and recording Elvis Presley songs in Latin with titles including *nunc hic aut numquam* ('It's Now Or Never'), *non adamare non possum* ('Can't Help Falling In Love'), *cor ligneum* ('Wooden Heart'), *tenere me ama* ('Love Me Tender'), *nunc distrahor* ('All Shook Up'), *ne saevias* ('Don't Be Cruel') and *gaudi calcei* ('Blue Suede Shoes').

Surely it's just a matter of time before someone turns their attention to the Beatles (*coleopteri*). So just in case here are title suggestions for all their official UK single releases...

ama me/ames me 'Love Me Do'
si tibi placet, me delecta 'Please Please Me'
a me, tibi 'From Me To You'
ea te amat 'She Loves You'
tui manum tenere volo 'I Want To Hold Your Hand'
(pecunia) non potest emere mihi amorem 'Can't Buy Me Love'
longi diei nox 'A Hard Day's Night'

valeo 'I Feel Fine'

tessera ad vehendum 'Ticket To Ride'

adiuva! 'Help!'

tantum per unum diem aderat/solvere possumus 'Day Tripper/
   We Can Work It Out'

libelli scriptor 'Paperback Writer'

crocea navis quae sub aqua est/Helena Rigby 'Yellow Submarine/
   Eleanor Rigby'

via sestertius nomine/fragorum agri sempiterni 'Penny Lane/
   Strawberry Fields Forever'

amore nobis omnibus opus est 'All You Need Is Love'

salve, vale 'Hello Goodbye'

matrona Madonna 'Lady Madonna'

Iude 'Hey Jude'

carmen Ioannis Yokoque 'The Ballad Of John And Yoko'

redi 'Get Back'

aliquid/ iungite 'Something/Come Together'

sit 'Let It Be'

heri 'Yesterday'

carissima, te modo cupio 'Baby It's You'

liber sicut avis 'Free As A Bird'

verus amor 'Real Love'

LATIN IN THE CINEMA

An American Werewolf In London (1981)
Spread over the internet is a untrue rumour that Jenny Agutter's London flat is in Lupus Street, Pimlico because lupus means wolf in Latin.

Atonement (2007)
Juno Temple plays on the name of Army Ammo chocolate bars for soldiers by reciting '*amo, amas, amat …*'

Braveheart (1995)
'*sanguinarius homo indomitus est*', kindly but rather loosely translated in the subtitles as 'He's a bloody murdering savage' is spoken by one Englishman to another in front of Mel Gibson (William Wallace) to describe him. The speaker is unaware that the educated Wallace understands perfectly and fashions a reply in the same secret tongue.

The Browning Version (1994)
Classics teacher Albert Finney quotes from Ovid's *ars*

amatoria: 'ars est celare artem' – the skill lies in how to hide the skill.

Carry On Cleo (1964)

Kenneth Williams translates his motto to clean up Rome, *'nihil ex pectore in omnibus'* as 'No spitting on public transport', neatly anticipating the later abbreviation of omnibus to bus by nearly two thousand years. A more literal translation would be 'nothing out of the chest on all people.'

The Da Vinci Code (2006)

'rhetor, omnes quattuor sunt mortui,' begins Paul Bettany on his mobile to his lords and masters of the *Opus Dei* in their preferred language. 'Teacher, all four (*senechaux*) are dead'... before ending with *'castigo meum corpus'* and some grim self-flagellation to chastise his body.

Dead Poets Society (1989)

'carpe diem', said the Roman poet Horace, 'because one shouldn't bet on tomorrow.' This was Robin Williams' philosophy to his English class. Oddly enough he had made a film called *Seize The Day* (1986) three years

earlier. And there are in-jokes in other Williams films *Mrs Doubtfire* (1993) and *Hook* (1991).

The same film features a Latin class declining the noun *agricola*, with the case order differing from the European way.

Empire Of The Sun (1987)

Doctor Nigel Havers tests young Christian Bale with 'I shall love', 'They were being loved' and 'I shall have been loved' to keep up spirits in a Japanese internment camp. Later on a forced march Bale keeps himself going by reciting the perfect indicative passive of *amo*.

Event Horizon (1997)

A doomed space-captain left a crackly broadcast for his failed rescuers to decipher. '*liberate tute me ex inferis. ave atque vale.*' *inferis* is the hell a nasty alien has put him in and *libero* here means deliver. This certainly caught someone's imagination as it appeared as a street wall graffito in Hammersmith in the late 90s.

Excalibur (1982)
'*lacimae mundi*, the tears of the world.' Nicol Williamson discusses the art of prophecy with Helen Mirren.

Fear In the Night (1972)
Headmaster Peter Cushing plays recordings in his school of pupils reciting *amatus sum, amatus es, amatus est* …The perfect indicative passive again.

Garfield 2 (2006)
The motto seen is *adeo vices parum efficio*. Never translated, it could mean a number of things, perhaps 'I address changes, I accomplish very little'.

The Grass Is Greener (1960)
Cary Grant quotes Terence's '*nil dictum quod non dictum prius.*' There's nothing said that hasn't been said before.

Greystoke (1984)
Note the Latin lesson Andie MacDowell (Jane) is giving Christopher Lambert (Tarzan). On the board is the future perfect of *amo*. No wonder, a cynic might observe, Tarzan couldn't wait to return to the jungle.

Hot Fuzz (2007)

Simon Pegg interrupts a meeting of the sinister village preservation society chanting *'bonum commune communitatis'* – the common good of the community.

Lara Croft: Tomb Raider (2001)

Iain Glen, quoting Virgil, says to Daniel Craig, *'tempus fugit'*, which Angelina Jolie then translates as the popular 'Time flies' though 'Time flees' is more accurate.

Lawrence Of Arabia (1962)

'Well *nil nisi bonum*. But did he really deserve a place in here?' sniffs a clergyman to Anthony Quayle, referring to St Paul's Cathedral. He is paraphrasing *de mortuis nil nisi bonum dicendum est* first quoted by Diogenes Laertius. One should speak only good of the dead.

Man Without A Face (1993)

Disfigured teacher Mel Gibson's philosophy to his young pupil Nick Stahl is *'aut disce aut discede.'* Learn or leave. Gibson asks Stahl to look up the Latin for his favourite attributive and he comes up with *excrementum* while *puer stultus* is given to geometry problems. Later on a hike Gibson tests Stahl with '*quidam magistri discipulos tanta cum arte docebant ut ipsi a discipulis quidem discerent*', which Stahl never quite finishes translating as 'certain masters teach their pupils with such great art that they themselves indeed learn from their pupils'.

The Matrix (1999)

'*temet nosce*' appears above the door when Keanu Reeves visits 'the oracle'. *temet* is an emphatic form of *te*, hence 'Know thyself'. How wise. The original is inscribed on the temple of Apollo at Delphi, γνωθι σεαυτον.

Monty Python's Life Of Brian (1979)

Romani, ite domum is the correct version demanded to be written out a hundred times by John Cleese as a Roman centurion, after Graham Chapman has painted the mural graffito *Romanes eunt domus*. Everything wrong there, declension of noun, mood of verb and no case ending for *domus*.

My House In Umbria (2003)

'*carpe diem*,' yup that one again, Ronnie Barker advises Maggie Smith.

Night Of The Lepus (1972)
A lepus is a hare and these are giant killers! Best categorised as cult fare.

The Omen (1976)
Remember the scary Gregorian chant? The words, as far as I can make out, are *'sanguis, bibimus, corpus, edimus, tolle corpus Satani ave, ave ave versus Cristus.'* The blood, we drink, the body, we eat, raise the body of Satan, hail, hail, anti Christ. Rather grim.

On Her Majesty's Secret Service (1968)
At the Royal College of Arms George Baker reveals to George Lazenby the Bond coat of arms, *orbis non sufficit* which of course lends its title to The World Is Not Enough.

Paint Your Wagon (1970)
Stretching it a bit but listen to the song 'Gospel Of No Name City' … 'Sodom was vice and *vice versa*. You wanna say where the vice was worser.'

The Passion Of The Christ (2004)

All of this film co-written, produced and directed by Mel Gibson dealing with the last hours of Jesus' cruci-fixion by Pontius Pilate in the 30s AD is in Aramaic and Latin.

Poseidon (2006)

Richard Dreyfuss orders an expensive bottle of wine with, yes, that one again, *'carpe diem'*.

The Princess Diaries (2001) and *The Princess Diaries 2* (2004)

The motto of Genovia, first seen briefly in the first film and a lot in the sequel, is *totus corpus laborat*. Oh dear, this understandable error is rather indicative of the perception that everything is Latin should end 'us'. Unfortunately *corpus* is a third declension neuter noun so it should be *totum corpus laborat* to mean 'the whole body works'.

Quo Vadis (1951)

The most famous version, as the others, takes its title from Peter's question, 'Whither goest thou?' to the Lord just before his crucifixion at Rome, as related in the apocryphal Acts Of Peter. Jesus' reply is '*eo Romam iterum crucifigi*' – 'I go to Rome to be crucified again'.

Sebastiane (1976)

Derek Jarman shot the whole of his film depicting the martyrdom of Sebastiane in the third century AD. entirely in Latin. Hardly a family film, the reason why most of the cast parade around naked is because the budget couldn't stretch to Roman uniforms.

Seconds (1966)

Old buddies Rock Hudson and Murray Hamilton recognise each other after plastic surgery with the key words '*fidelis aeternus*' – eternally faithful.

The Silence Of The Lambs (1993)

'*quid pro quo*, Clarice,' utters Anthony Hopkins to Jodie Foster. Something for something.

Tombstone (1993)

Unusual in a western, there is a witty trade of Latin aphorisms threateningly expressed by Val Kilmer (Doc

Holliday) and Michael Biehn (Ringo) in Wyatt Earp's bar. A very free translation is provided.

Doc: *in vino veritas.* You're drunk. (from Pliny)
Ringo: *age quid agis.* A man's gotta do … (proverb)
Doc: *credat judaeus Apella. non ego.*
Who are you kidding? (from Horace)
Ringo: *eventus stultorum magister*
You'll be wise after the event. (Livy)
Doc: *in pace requiescat.* You're dead. (Latin Mass)

The Truman Show (1998)
omnes pro uno, unum pro omnibus is the motto of Seaside, Jim Carrey's TV town in Florida. Translated means 'all for one, one for all.'

V for Vendetta (2005)
Natalie Portman reads out '*vi veri veniversum vivus vici,*' which Hugo Weaving correctly translates as 'By the power of truth, I, while living, have conquered the universe' but then blows it by saying it's from *Faust* by Goethe when it is thought it's Marlowe's *Doctor Faustus*. John Standing chips in with a '*mea culpa*'.

Victim (1961)

Sinister Derren Nesbitt threatens Dirk Bogarde with Juvenal's *'mens sana in corpore sano'* though if one listens carefully, he seems to say, *'mens sano in corporae sana.'*

Vice Versa (1948) and Vice Versa (1988)

Two of the several adaptations of F. Anstey's body-swap Victorian novel. A good example of assimilation into English with this phrase generally understood as 'and the other way around'.

The Wizard Of Oz (1939)

Wizard Frank Morgan confers a degree of Thinkology from the *Universitatus Comitiatum e pluribus unum* (a very thinly veiled USA reference) to scarecrow Ray Bolger.

Young Winston (1972)

After perfectly declining *mensa* Winston Churchill's famous bewilderment over the vocative case, especially when invoking a table, is re-enacted word for word as described in *My Early Life* by young Russell Lewis and headmaster Robert Hardy.

And to finish with, an excerpt from TV's *The West Wing,*

and an episode entitled 'Two Cathedrals' where president Jebediah Bartlett (Martin Sheen) enjoys a sarcastic rant against God in a cathedral:

> **gratias tibi ago, Domine. haec credam a Deo pio, a Deo iusto, a Deo scito. cruciatus in crucem. tuus in terra servus, nuntius fui: officium effeci. cruciatus in crucem. eas in crucem.**

TRANSLATION:
Thanks a lot, Lord. Am I to believe these acts came from a righteous God, a just God, an omniscient God? Go to hell. I have been your servant, your messenger on this earth. I did my duty. Be crucified on the cross. May you go to hell.

A little bit of latin...

How does one measure intelligence?
Whenever the question arises over the intelligence of England and Chelsea midfielder Frank Lampard, a fact supporting he is the brightest professional footballer in the business is his A* in GCSE Latin. Say no more.

QUIZ I: JAMES BOND FILMS

You won't need any help with these, though some of
the Ian Fleming titles are a challenge even in English.
They're in chronological order, but include the two
non-official titles.

medicus minime
a sinistra civitate (cum) amore
digitus auri
globus tonitrus
bis solum vivis
regius locus in quo ludi pecuniae tenentur
in servitudine secreto pro regina (I.S.S.P.R.)
pretiosae lapides sunt aeternae
vivet et moriatur
vir aureo telo
explorator qui me amabat
vir qui lunae imaginem removere conatur, i.e. is qui impossi-
bile somnium petit
tuis oculis solum

animal cui sunt octo membra
numquam dic numquam iterum
consilium ad necandum/interficiendum
vivae luces diei
ei licet ut necet/occidat/interficiat
oculus aureus
cras numquam morietur
orbis terrarum haud satis est
morere alio die
regius locus in quo ludi pecuniae tenentur
minima quantitas solacii

Ancient Rome Monopoly

Even 75 years on, Monopoly still has no Latin version, so here is one based on Ancient Rome keeping in spirit with the original game and at times fairly random choices of streets and areas elected by Waddingtons, based in Leeds, for Parker Brothers.

Go *vade;* Old Kent Road *summoenium (area outside the centre);*
Whitechapel *macellum Liviae (shopping centre on the Esquiline);*
King's Cross Station *porta Aurelia (gate in the north-west);* The
Angel, Islington *media subura (like the Angel, an area rather than
a street, famed for nightlife, between the Equiline and Viminal
hills);* Euston Road *via Appia (first Roman road);* Pentonville
Road *alta semita ('high path,' passing over Quirinal);* Jail
Tullianum (the Mamertine prison named after king Tullius); Pall
Mall *via sacra (important central street);* Electric Company *excu-
bitorium vigilum (barracks of firefighters);* Whitehall *comitium
(political centre);* Northumberland Avenue *vicus Iugarius (runs
along the Capitol);* Marylebone Station *porta Capena (gate on via
Appia on Caelian hill running to south-east);* Bow Street *vicus
Tuscus (Etruscan central street near forum);* Marlborough Street
clivus Argentarius (as above); Vine Street *via nova (as above);* Free
parking *liberum spatium (a free space);* Strand *argiletum (street
specialising in books);* Fleet Street *vicus sandalarius (as above, cel-
ebrating the former newspaper street);* Trafalgar Square *basilica
Iulia (court decorated with statues);* Fenchurch Street Station
porta salaria ('salt' gate to north); Leicester Square *circus maximus (city's premium entertainment);* Coventry Street *lacus pasto-
rum (pond of the shepherds, very random);* Water works *clo ca*

*maxima (the main drain to the Tiber);*Piccadilly Circus *miliarium aureum (the forum's golden milestone, similar to 'Eros');* Go to jail *vade ad Tullianum;* Regent Street *via lata ('wide road,' now via del corso, very straight unlike Regent's bend);* Oxford Circus *via Flaminia (runs into the via lata);* Bond Street *saepta Iulia (enclosed public building near the via lata);* Liverpool Street Station *porta Esquilina (gate on the Esquiline to the east);* Park Lane *clivus Publicius (near the circus maximus);* Mayfair *mons Capitolinus (the heart of Rome and smallest hill);* Chance *sors (lot, fate);* Community Chest *civitatis arca (box of the state)*

N.B. IMPORTANCE OF STREETS RUNS ROUGHLY IN ORDER OF IMPORTANCE STARTING WITH *via, vicus, clivus,* DOWN TO *semita.*

ENGLISH PLACE NAMES

Most English place names have origins in Celtic, Anglo-Saxon and Old English and indeed Latin, though the Roman names from the time of imperial occupation have long gone. For example the Roman Deva is now Chester, itself owing its origins to Latin.

Places ending in -cester, e.g. Bicester, Chester, Winchester, and -caster, e.g. Lancaster, derive from *castra*, (a camp/fortifications) where a Roman legion built a camp and a settlement became permanent.

Ecclesia (church) is evident in Eccles, Lancashire.

Colonia, as in *Lindum Colonia*, survives in the Anglo-Saxon Lincoln. London seems to rather hang onto its old name of *Londinium* as a positive addition to its status. But there are many settlements which retain Latin today:

LATIN	MEANING AND ENGLISH PLACE
abbas	ABBOT: MILTON, MELBURY, COMPTON (ALL DORSET)
ambo	BOTH: LILLINGS AMBO (YORKS) I.E. BOTH WEST AND EAST LILLINGS
canonicorum	OF THE CLERGYMEN: WHITCHURCH CANONICORUM (DORSET)
cum	WITH: NYLAND CUM BATCOMBE (SOMERSET), ISLEY CUM LANGLEY (LEICS.), HEADON CUM UPTON (NOTTS.), ESKDALESIDE CUM UGGLEBARNBY (YORKS.)
ducis	OF THE DUKE OR DUKES (ALTERNATIVE NOMINATIVE PLURAL): COLLINGBOURNE DUCIS (WILTS)
episcopi	OF THE BISHOP (HERE OF BATH AND WELLS): HUISH (WHICH MEANS LANDS NOT SOME MANGLED VERSION OF

LATIN	MEANING AND ENGLISH PLACE
	HIC HAEC HOC) EPISCOPI, KINGSBURY EPISCOPI (BOTH SOMERSET)
extra and infra	OUTSIDE AND WITHIN: ROMSEY EXTRA ENCIRCLES ROMSEY INFRA WHOSE BORDERS DEPEND ON A BRIDGE (HANTS)
forum	MARKET PLACE: BLANDFORD FORUM (DORSET)
fratrum	OF THE BROTHERS: TOLLER (THE RIVER TOLLER IS NOW CALLED THE HOOKE), FRATRUM (DORSET)
in fabis	IN BEANS: BARTON IN FABIS, GUESS THE VILLAGE'S PRODUCE, (NOTTS)
inferior	LOWER: TABLEY INFERIOR (CHESHIRE)
intrinseca	INTERNAL: RYME INTRINSECA (DORSET). THERE WAS AN EXTRINSECA BUT NO MORE. 'DORSET' BY SIR JOHN BETJEMAN STARTS 'RYME INTRINSECA ...'
iuxta / juxta	CLOSE TO: NORTON J. TWYCROSS (LEICS), BRADFORD J. COGGESHALL, TILBURY J. CLARE (BOTH ESSEX)
longa	LONG: STOW (WHICH IS OLD ENGLISH FOR HOLY PLACE), LONGA (CAMBS)
magna	GREAT: APPLEBY MAGNA, STRETTON MAGNA (BOTH LEICS.), ASTON MAGNA, COMPTON MAGNA (BOTH GLOS.), HAMPTON MAGNA (WARKS.), CHEW (A RIVER) MAGNA (SOMERSET), FONTMELL MAGNA (DORSET)
monachorum	OF THE MONKS: BUCKLAND MONACHORUM (DEVON)
parva	SMALL: APPLEBY PARVA, STRETTON PARVA (BOTH LEICS.)
porcorum	OF THE PIGS: TOLLER PORCORUM (DORSET)
puerorum	OF THE BOYS: ASHBY PUERORUM (LINCS.)
sub	UNDER: NORTON SUB HAMDON (SOMERSET), ASTON SUB EDGE, WESTON SUB EDGE (BOTH GLOS.)
super mare	ABOVE THE SEA: WESTON SUPER MARE (SOMERSET) BUT PRONOUNCED MAIR RATHER THAN MA-RE.
superior	UPPER: TABLEY SUPERIOR (CHESHIRE)

UNITED STATES OF AMERICA

In 1782, after six years of scholarly thought, a great seal was completed to commerate the United States' independence. The seal's obverse contains *e pluribus unum*, out of many (states or peoples), one (nation or people). This phrase was originally thought to be a recipe for a dish of many ingredients. While it's often attributed to Virgil, the reverse mottoes definitely recall his work the Aeneid, *annuit coeptis* (he gave his approval to the undertakings) and the fourth Georgic, *novus ordo seculorum* (a new order of ages). These mottoes can be seen on the back of the US dollar bill while *e pluribus unum* is on all the cent, nickel, dime and quarter coins.

Several American states have adopted mottoes in Latin with Maryland and South Carolina even taking two.

US STATE MOTTOES

US STATE	MOTTO	TRANSLATION
ALABAMA	*audemus iura nostra defendere*	WE DARE DEFEND OUR RIGHTS
ALASKA	*ditat Deus*	GOD ENRICHES (GENESIS INSPIRED)
ARIZONA	*regnat populus*	THE PEOPLE RULE
CALIFORNIA	ευρηκα	I'VE FOUND IT (ARCHIMEDES) (YES, GREEK, BUT TOO GOOD TO OMIT)
COLORADO	*nil sine numine*	NOTHING WITHOUT DIVINE WILL (VIRGIL, ADAPTED)
CONNECTICUT	*qui transtulit sustinet*	HE WHO TRANSFERRED SUSTAINS (PSALMS, ADAPTED)
DELAWARE	*iustitia omnibus*	JUSTICE FOR ALL (LAST WORDS OF THE PLEDGE OF ALLEGIANCE)
IDAHO	*esto perpetua*	BE PERPETUAL (ORIGINALLY REFERRING TO VENICE)
KANSAS	*ad astra per aspera*	TO STARS THROUGH ADVERSITIES (RECALLS THE RAF MOTTO *per ardua ad astra*)
KENTUCKY	*Deo gratiam habeamus*	LET'S GIVE THANKS TO GOD (KENTUCKY'S MOTTO WAS ONLY ADOPTED IN 2002 SO LATIN LIVES ON INTO THE 21ST CENTURY)
MAINE	*dirigo*	I GUIDE
MINNESOTA	*ense petit placidam sub libertate quietem*	WITH THE SWORD SHE SEEKS PEACE UNDER LIBERTY
MARYLAND	*crescite et multipli-camini*	GROW AND MULTIPLY (GENESIS)
	scuto bonae voluntatis tuae coro-nasti nos	YOU'VE CROWNED US WITH THE SHIELD OF YOUR GOODWILL (PSALMS)
MISSISSIPPI	*ni si quaeris peninsulam amoenam*	IF YOU SEEK A PLEASANT PENINSULA, LOOK AROUND (RECALLS THE CHRISTOPHER WREN INSCRIPTION IN

LATIN MATTERS

US STATE	MOTTO	TRANSLATION
MASSACHUSETTS	*circumspice*	ST PAUL'S CATHEDRAL, LONDON) WITH COURAGE AND ARMS
MONTANA	*virtute et armis* *salus populi suprema lex esto*	LET THE WELFARE OF THE PEOPLE BE THE SUPREME LAW (ALSO THE MOTTO OF THE LONDON BOROUGH OF LEWISHAM AND CAN BE FOUND ON THE LIBRARY IN WALWORTH ROAD WHICH IS IN SOUTHWARK)
NEW MEXICO	*crescit eundo*	IT GROWS AS IT GOES
NEW YORK	*excelsior*	HIGHER (LONGFELLOW)
NORTH CAROLINA	*esse quam videri*	TO BE RATHER THAN SEEM (CICERO)
OHIO	*imperium in imperio*	EMPIRE WITHIN AN EMPIRE (OHIO'S WAS VERY SHORT-LIVED, LASTING ONLY A COUPLE OF YEARS IN THE NINETEENTH CENTURY)
OKLAHOMA	*labor omnia vincit*	WORK CONQUERS ALL (VIRGIL)
OREGON	*alis volat propriis*	SHE FLIES WITH HER OWN WINGS
SOUTH CAROLINA	*animis opibusque parati dum spiro, spero*	READY IN MIND AND RESOURCES WHILE I LIVE, I HOPE (ATTRIBUTED TO CICERO)
VIRGINIA	*sic semper tyrannis*	THUS ALWAYS TO TYRANTS (APPARENTLY QUOTED BY JOHN WILKES BOOTH WHEN HE SHOT ABRAHAM LINCOLN)
WEST VIRGINIA	*montani semper liberi*	MOUTAINEERS ARE ALWAYS FREE
WYOMING	*arma togae cedant*	LET ARMS YIELD TO THE TOGA (CICERO)

Football Mottoes

A few English and Scottish clubs in the premiership, championship and lower divisions sport Latin mottoes on their club crests. These crests occasionally find their way into the design of players' shirts, though annual, and money-making, renewal of these designs can mean the omission of the crest from one year to another.

Arsenal:
victoria concordia crescit (victory grows from agreement, i.e. harmony breeds victory)
victoria is nominative but *concordia* ablative.

Everton:
nil satis nisi optimum (nothing enough unless the best, i.e. only the best will do)
This is similar to the Northern Irish side Ballyclare's *nihil nisi optimi*.

Blackburn Rovers:
arte et labore (with skill and hard work)
  Both nouns are third declension ablatives.

Manchester City:
superbia in proelio (with pride in battle)
  superbia is probably ablative but could be nominative to mean simply 'pride in battle'.

Tottenham Hotspur:
audere est facere (to dare is to do, i.e. daring is doing)
  The verbs are infinitive showing a nice classical preference to nominative gerunds.

Sheffield Wednesday:
consilio et animis (with a plan and minds, i.e. with wisdom and courage)
  Both nouns are ablative, *consilio* singular, *animis* plural.

Tranmere Rovers:
ubi fides ibi lux et robur (where faith there light and strength, i.e. where there is belief, therein lies light and strength)

Bury:

vincit omnia industria (hard work overcomes everything)

The first declension noun *industria* is nominative singular but *omnia* is accusative plural neuter.

Bristol City:

vim promovet insitam (promotes innate power)

This motto is shared with Bristol University and taken from Horace's 4th Ode which reveals that *doctrina* (learning) is the promoter of inner power.

The adjective *insitam's* –am ending rather than –um reveals the noun *vim's* gender as feminine.

Gillingham:

domus clamantium (house of those shouting, i.e home to vocal support)

clamantium is a genitive plural present participle active used as a substantive. Now that's worth shouting about.

Mossley:

floret qui laborat (he who works flourishes)

Many mottoes rely on a 'He who' translation for *qui* rather than merely 'who'.

Kilmarnock:
confidemus (we shall trust, i.e. we trust)
  The verb is future simple.

Elgin City:
sic itur ad astra (thus one goes to the stars, i.e. we aim high)
  itur is an impersonal passive from the verb *eo. astra* is accusative plural neuter given away by the fact that *ad* governs the accusative.

Queens Park:
ludere causa ludendi (playing for the sake of playing)
  Note the neat contrast of infinitive standing in for a nominative gerund with a gerund in the genitive.

Clydebank:
labore et scientia (by work and knowledge)
  More ablatives.

ASTERIX

This endearing and enduring comic book series written and illustrated by Rene Goscinny (until his death in 1977) and Albert Uderzo frequently drew on well-known Latin phrases, usually untranslated and quoted by Roman legionaries, Julius Caesar and a particularly literate peg-legged pirate. Below are the quotations from all 33 books and the source if known. Many of these come from Peter Kessler's *Complete Guide*.

ab imo pectore (from the bottom of the heart)
   A quotation from Caesar, *Asterix and the Chieftian's Shield*

acta est fabula (The story is done)
   Augustus's dying words, *Asterix and the Golden Sickle*

alea iacta est (The die is cast)
   Caesar crossing the Rubicon, *Asterix the Gladiator*

audaces fortuna iuvat (Fortune favours the bold)
Virgil using *audentes* (those daring) instead of
audaces, Asterix and the Chieftian's Shield.

auri sacra fames (The cursed hunger for gold)
Virgil, *Asterix and the Roman Agent*

aut Caesar aut nihil (Either Caesar or nothing)
Cesare Borgia's motto, *Asterix the Gaul*

ave atque vale (Hail and farewell)
Catullus , *Asterix and the Black Gold*

beati pauperes spiritu (Blessed are the poor in spirit)
St Matthew's Gospel , *Asterix in Spain*

bis repetita placent (Those things that please are
rehashed again and again)
Horace, *Asterix and the Chieftian's Shield*

carpe diem (Seize the day)
On a sign advising 'Be brief', Horace, *Asterix and
the Chieftain's Shield*

caveat emptor (Let the buyer beware)
    Asterix and the Great Divide, Asterix and the Actress

ceterarum rerum prudens (Wary of everything else)
    Cicero adapted, *Asterix and the Actress*

cogito ergo sum (I think therefore I am)
    Descartes , *Asterix the Legionary*

contraria contrariis curantur (Opposites are cured
    by opposites)
    Hippocrates, *Asterix and the Magic Carpet*

de facto (In fact)
    Asterix the Gaul

de mortuis nil nisi bonus ([Say] nothing but good
    of the dead)
    Attributed by Diogenes to Chilon, *Asterix and
    Caesar's Gift*

delenda Carthago [est] (Carthage must be destroyed)
    Cato, *Asterix and the Laurel Wreath*

desinit in piscem mulier formosa superne (A woman, beautiful above, ends in a fishtail below)
Horace, *Asterix and the Secret Weapon*

diem perdidi (I have lost the day)
Titus bemoaning a wasted day, *Asterix and the Chieftain's Shield*

dignus est intrare (He is worthy to enter)
Moliere, *Asterix the Legionary*

dulce et decorum est pro patria mori (It is sweet and fitting to die for one's country)
Horace, *Asterix and the Big Fight*

errare humanum est (To err is human)
Seneca , *Asterix and the Goths*

et nunc, reges, intelligite, erudimini, qui iudicati terram (And now, kings, understand, be taught, you who have judged the Earth)
Nice juxtaposition of active and passive imperatives from Psalms, *Asterix and the Olympic Games*

et tu, Brute (Even you, Brutus?)
    Caesar's dying words according to Plutarch, *Asterix
    the Gladiator*, variation *et tu Asterix* in *Asterix and
    Caesar's Gift*

exegi monumentum aere perennius (I have raised
    a monument more lasting than bronze)
    Horace at his least modest, *Asterix and the Banquet*

felix qui potuit rerum cognoscere causas (Happy
    is he who could learn the causes of things)
    Virgil, *Asterix All At Sea*

fluctuat nec mergitur (It wavers but it does not sink)
    motto of Paris, *Asterix in Britain*

gloria victis (Glory to the defeated)
    Asterix and the Lauren Wreath

hic haec hoc (This [nominative masc./fem./neut.])
    declined by drunken Roman legionaries, *Asterix in
    Britain*

ipso facto (By the very fact)
  Asterix the Gaul

ira furor brevis est (Anger is a brief madness)
  Horace, *Asterix and the Great Crossing*

ita diis placuit (Thus it pleased the gods)
  Asterix and Cleopatra

legio expedita (Legion, attention!)
  Asterix and Caesar's Gift

maior e longinquo reverentia (Greater reverence
  from afar)
  Asterix in Switzerland

mea culpa (My fault)
  Asterix and the Class Act

mens sana in corpore sano (A sound mind in a
  sound body)
  Juvenal, *Asterix and the Olympic Games*

mensa, mensa, mensam, mensae, mensae, mensa
[declension of table, heard from Berlix's School of
Modern languages in *Asterix and the Big Fight*]

morituri te salutant (Those who are about to die
salute you)
Suetonius, *'Asterix the Gladiator'*, a singular version
moriturus te saluto (I about to salute you) in *Asterix
in Belgium* and a variation *lucratori* (Those about to
get rich) in *Asterix and the Black Gold*

nihil conveniens decretis eius (Nothing fitting to his
decrees)
Cicero , *Asterix and the Falling Sky*

non licet omnibus adire Corinthum (Not everyone
may go to Corinth)
Horace, *Asterix in Belgium*

non omnia possumus omnes (We cannot all [do]
everything)
Virgil , *Asterix and the Black Gold*

nunc dimittis (Now you depart)
St. Luke's Gospel, *Asterix and the Great Divide*

nunc est bibendum (Now there's drinking to be done)
Horace, 'Asterix in Switzerland'

o fortunatos nimium, sua si bona norint agricolas
(What fortunate farmers, if they only knew their good lot)
Virgil, *Asterix in Britain*

o tempora, o mores (What times! What customs!)
Cicero, *Asterix and the Chieftain's Shield*

panem et circenses (Bread and circuses)
Juvenal, *Asterix and the Chieftain's Shield*

pax Romana: (Roman Peace)
Asterix and the Golden Sickle

plaudite cives! (Applaud, citizens!)
Asterix the Gladiator

qualis artifex pereo (As what a [good] artist I die)
    Nero's dying words according to Suetonius, *Asterix and the Secret Weapon*

qui habet aures audiendi audiat (He who has ears, let him hear)
    St. Mark's Gospel *Asterix and Caesar's Gift*

quid novi? (What's new?)
    Asterix the Gaul variation with nice vocative of 'filius, quid novi, fili', *Asterix and the Secret Weapon*

quid pro quo (something in return),
    Asterix and the Cauldron

quis, quod, ubi, quibus auxiliis, cur, quomodo, quando? (Who, what, where, in what ways, why, how, when?)
    Quintilian, *Asterix and the Golden Sickle*

quo vadis? (Whither goest thou?)
    St. John's Gospel, *Asterix and the Laurel Wreath* with addition domine in *Asterix and the Class Act*

quod erat demonstrandum (That to be proved
[has been])
Asterix and Son

quomodo vales? (How are you?)
Asterix the Legionary

quot capita, tot sensus (As many feelings as heads)
Asterix and the Magic Carpet

quousque tandem? (How long?)
Cicero, *Mansion of the Gods*

redde Caesari quae sunt Caesaris (Render unto
Caesar the things that are Caesar's)
St. Matthew's Gospel, *Obelox and Co*

res non verba (deeds not words)
Asterix and the Class Act

resquiescamus in pace (Let's rest in peace)
Asterix and the Great Divide

ruber et niger (Red and black)
    card game, *Asterix and the Chieftain's Shield*

si vis pacem [para bellum] (If you wish peace,
    [be ready for war])
    Flavius Vegetius, *Obelix and Co*

sic ad nauseam (Thus to the point of nausea)
    Asterix and Son

sic transit gloria [mundi] (Thus passes away the
    glory [of the world])
    Uttered during a papal coronation to remind the
    Pope of his mortality, *Asterix and the Normans*

signa inferre! praege! concursu! ad gladios! infestis pilis!
    (Bring on banners, forward, in a charge, to swords,
    with pilums at ready)
    Asterix and Son

singularis porcus (Wild boar)
    Linnaeus' classification, *Asterix the Gladiator*

sol lucet omnibus (The sun shines for everyone),
  Petronius, *Asterix and the Normans*

summum jus, summa injuria (the utmost
  enactment of law, the utmost injustice)
  Cicero, *Asterix All At Sea*

sursum corda (Lift up your hearts)
  Roman Catholic versicle, *Asterix the Gaul*

timeo Danaos et dona ferentes (I fear Greeks
  even when bearing gifts)
  Virgil, *Asterix the Legionary*

ubi solitudinem faciunt, pacem appellant (Where
  they make desolation, they call it peace)
  Tacitus, *Asterix and the Cauldron*

uti, non abuti (To use, not abuse)
  Obelix and Co

vade retro (Get thee behind me)
Terence and later St. Mark's Gospel, *Asterix and the Golden Sickle*

vae victo, vae victis (Woe to the vanquished man, woe to the vanquished men)
Livy, *Asterix the Gaul*

vanitas vanitatum et omnia vanitas (Vanity of vanities, all [is] vanity)
Ecclesiastes, *Asterix in Spain*

veni vidi vici (I came, I saw, I conquered)
Caesar according to Plutarch, *Asterix in Spain*

veritas odium parit (Truth begets hatred)
Terence, *Asterix and the Laurel Wreath*

victrix causa diis placuit, sed victa Catoni
(The victorious cause pleased the gods, the defeated one pleased Cato)
Lucan, Asterix and the Banquet

victurus te saluto (I, about to win, salute you)
    Asterix and the Big Fight

video meliora proboque deteriora sequor (I see
    and approve the better ways, but I follow the
    worse ones)
    Ovid, *Asterix and the Goths*

vinum et musica laetificant cor (Wine and music
    gladden the heart)
    Asterix and Caesar's Gift

vis comica (comic power)
    Suetonius quoting Caesar on Terence, *Asterix and
    the Great Crossing*

A little bit of latin...

The pound in your pocket

Current new pence boast in honour of Elizabeth II, D.G.REG.. F.D, or *dei gratia regina fidei defensor* – by the grace of God, queen and defender of the faith.

The English pound coin's edge reveals *decus et tutamen* (honour and protection, used as a reassurance that the coin isn't clipped as they used to be in the 17th century when the phrase was first used on a coin) comes from Virgil's Aeneid V and the full line is *donat habere viro, decus et tutamen in armis.*

QUIZ II: NUMBER ONE HITS

IDENTIFY THE HIT RECORDS

All reached No. 1 in the UK singles chart and received constant airplay thanks to re-releases, covers, inclusion in films and advertising use. The names of acts and years they reached the top are provided as enormous clues. Some are literally translated so may need further manipulation.

Year	NUMBER ONE HIT
1953	*credo* (FRANKIE LAINE; ROBSON & JEROME, 1995)
1954	*tres denarii in fonte* (FRANK SINATRA)
1955	*'liberatum e vinculis' carmen* (JIMMY YOUNG; RIGHTEOUS BROTHERS, 1990; ROBSON & JEROME, 1995; GARETH GATES, 2002)
1956	*est paene cras* (THE DREAMWEAVERS)
1957	*erit ille dies [in quo moriar]* (THE CRICKETS)
1958	*magni globi ignis* (JERRY LEE LEWIS)
1959	*quid vis?* (ADAM FAITH)
1960	*solum soli* (ROY ORBISON)
1961	*ad me recta redi* (EVERLY BROTHERS)
1962	*terra mira* (THE SHADOWS)

Year	NUMBER ONE HIT
1963	*quomodo id efficis?* (GERRY AND THE PACEMAKERS)
1964	*domus solis orientis* (THE ANIMALS), *magnopere cepisti* (THE KINKS)
1965	*i nunc* (MOODY BLUES), *mihi non satis est* (ROLLING STONES)
1966	*hae caligae factae sunt ad ambulandum* (NANCY SINATRA), *viridianae herbae domi* (TOM JONES)
1967	*hoc est meum carmen* (PETULA CLARK), *libera me* (ENGELBERT HUMPERDINCK), *silentium est aureum* (TREMELOES)
1968	*quam orbem mirabilem* (LOIUS ARMSTRONG; EVA CASSIDY & KATIE MELUA, 2007), *mihi tibi nuntiandum est* (BEE GEES), *parvo auxilio ab meis amicis* (JOE COCKER; WET WET WET, 1988)
1969	*quo vadis, mea pulchra?* (PETER SARSTEDT)
1970	*omnia genera omnium* (DANA), *anulus auri* (FREDA PAYNE)
1971	*calidus amor* (T. REX)
1972	*sine te* (NILSSON; MARIAH CAREY, 1994), *quomodo confirmari possum?* (DAVID CASSIDY)
1973	*flava vitta antiquam quercum circumligate* (DAWN)
1974	*illa* (CHARLES AZNAVOUR), *quando iterum te videbis?* (THE THREE DEGREES)
1975	*si* (TELLY SAVALAS), *navigo* (ROD STEWART)
1976	*retine mihi omnia basia* (BROTHERHOOD OF MAN)
1977	*itaque iterum vincis* (HOT CHOCOLATE)
1978	*ter femina* (THE COMMODORES), *aetatis noctes* (JOHN TRAVOLTA & OLIVIA NEWTON-JOHN)
1979	*clari oculi* (ART GARFUNKEL), *nuntius in amphora* (THE POLICE)
1980	*victor omnia vincit* (ABBA)
1981	*mulier* (JOHN LENNON), *nonne me cupis?* (HUMAN LEAGUE)
1983	*verus* (SPANDAU BALLET)

Year	NUMBER ONE HITS
1984	*sciuntne diem natalem esse?* (BAND AID, ALSO 1989, 2004)
1985	*volo scire quid sit amor* (FOREIGNER),
	move propius (PHYLLIS NELSON)
1986	*noli relinquere me hoc modo* (COMMUNARDS)
1987	*iterum vincis* (BEE GEES),
	quis est illa puella? (MADONNA)
1988	*is non gravis est, ille est meus frater* (HOLLIES),
	tibi nihil debeo (BROS), *perfectus* (FAIRGROUND ATTRACTION),
	Olympus est locus, qui est in terra (BELINDA CARLISLE)
1989	*aeterna flamma* (BANGLES; ATOMIC KITTEN, 2001)
1990	*nihil te assimulat* (SINEAD O'CONNOR)
1991	*omnia quae facio, pro te ago* (BRYAN ADAMS)
1992	*finis viae* (BOYZ II MEN), *te semper amabo* (WHITNEY HOUSTON)
1994	*ubique est amor* (WET WET WET), *mane alium diem* (EAST 17)
1995	*villa* (BLUR)
1996	*noli respectare, irate* (OASIS), *tres leones* (LIGHTNING SEEDS, AGAIN IN
	1998), *vis esse* (SPICE GIRLS), *verba* (BOYZONE)
1997	*noli loqui* (NO DOUBT), *candela in vento* (ELTON JOHN),
1998	*numquam umquam* (ALL SAINTS), *cors meum supererit* (CELINE DION)
1999	*volans sine alis* (WESTLIFE)
2000	*eheu ... iterum egi* (BRITNEY SPEARS)
2002	*si cras numquam adveniat* (RONAN KEATING)
2003	*pulchra* (CHRISTIAN AGUILERA)
2004	*tibi faveo* (GIRLS ALOUD)
2005	*adeone Amarillo?* (TONY CHRISTIE), *es bella* (JAMES BLUNT), *me tollis*
	(WESTLIFE)
2006	*mihi ridendum est* (LILY ALLEN), *mihi saltare non placet* (SCISSOR SISTERS)
2007	*quingenta milia passuum* (THE PROCLAIMERS)

ENGLISH COUNTIES

The counties of England have been rearranged throughout the centuries – most recently in 1965, 1974 and 1996 – but the mottoes have survived by and large as counties come and go. Nicely summing up the confusion is the sole Welsh county to have a Latin motto. Pembrokeshire was merged into Dyfed in 1974, but returned in 1996 as Pembrokeshire with its motto *ex unitate vires* (from unity strength) intact.

Here is a list of counties, some of which are ceremonial and others currently obsolete, but which, one never knows, may return.

COUNTY	MOTTO	TRANSLATION
BUCKINGHAMSHIRE	*vestigia nulla retrorsum*	NO BACKWARD STEP (HORACE ADAPTED)
CAMBRIDGESHIRE	*corde uno sapientes simus per undas per agros sapientes simus*	WITH ONE HEART LET US BE WISE THROUGH WAVES, THROUGH FIELDS LET US BE WISE
CHESHIRE	*iure et dignitate gladii*	BY RIGHT AND DIGNITY OF THE SWORD
CUMBERLAND	*perfero*	I CARRY OUT
CUMBRIA	*ad montes oculos levavi*	I LIFTED MY EYES TO THE HILLS

COUNTY	MOTTO	TRANSLATION
DERBYSHIRE	*bene consulendo*	BY COUNSELLING WELL
DEVON	*auxilio divino*	WITH DIVINE HELP
GLOUCESTER	*prorsum semper*	EVER ONWARDS
HEREFORDSHIRE	*pulchra terra Dei donum*	THIS BEAUTIFUL LAND IS GOD'S GIFT
HUNTINGDONSHIRE	*labore omnia florent*	EVERYTHING FLOURISHES WITH WORK
KENT	*invicta*	UNBEATEN
LANCASHIRE	*in concilio consilium*	IN COUNCIL WISDOM
LONDON, CITY OF	*Domine, dirige nos*	LORD, DIRECT US
NORTH YORKSHIRE	*unitate fortior*	STRONGER UNITED
NORTHAMPTONSHIRE	*rosa concordiae signum*	THE ROSE IS THE SIGN OF HARMONY
NOTTINGHAMSHIRE	*sapienter proficiens*	WISELY ADVANCING
OXFORDSHIRE	*sapere aude*	DARE TO KNOW
RUTLAND	*multum in parvo*	MUCH IN A LITTLE
SHROPSHIRE	*floreat Salopia*	MAY SHROPSHIRE FLOURISH
SUFFOLK	*opus nostrum dirige*	DIRECT OUR WORK

A little bit of latin...

Dry humour

After he'd ordered a bottle of Hock in a restaurant, a Latin *magister* absent-mindedly added, '*hic, haec, hoc, hunc, hanc, hoc ...*' When the wine still hadn't arrived twenty minutes later, he called over the waiter, asking, 'Didn't I order Hock?'

'Yes, sir,' replied the witty waiter, 'but then you declined it.'

UNIVERSITY MOTTOES

Educational mottoes are sometimes in Latin, often religious and always optimistic, in an attempt to grab the aspirations and imagination of their students. It sometimes works. Here a just a few British examples from the thousands over the world including the *alma mater* of the odd Prime Minister or several. See if you can spot them...

UNIVERSITY	MOTTO	TRANSLATION
ABERDEEN	*initium sapientiae timor Domini:*	FEAR OF THE LORD IS THE BEGINNING OF WISDOM (ECCLESIASTICUS)
BIRMINGHAM	*per ardua ad alta:*	THROUGH HARD WORK, TO THE HEIGHTS
BRISTOL	*vim promovet insitam:*	PROMOTES INNATE POWER (HORACE)
CAMBRIDGE	*hinc lucem et pocula sacra:*	FROM HERE [WE DRAIN] THE LIGHT AND SACRED CUPS [OF KNOWLEDGE]
CHESTER	*qui docet in doctrina:*	HE WHO TEACHES, ON TEACHING (ROMANS)
DERBY	*experientia docet;*	EXPERIENCE TEACHES
DUNDEE	*magnificat anima mea dominum:*	MY SOUL MAGNIFIES THE LORD (LUKE)
DURHAM	*fundamenta eius super montibus sanctis:*	HER FOUNDATIONS [ARE] UPON THE HOLY HILLS (PSALMS)
EXETER	*lucem sequimur:*	WE FOLLOW THE LIGHT

LATIN MATTERS

UNIVERSITY	MOTTO	TRANSLATION
GLASGOW	via, veritas, vita	THE WAY, THE TRUTH, THE LIFE
LEEDS	et augebitur scientia	AND KNOWLEDGE WILL BE INCREASED
LEICESTER	ut vitam habeant	SO THAT THEY MAY HAVE LIFE (JOHN)
LINCOLN	excellentia per studium	EXCELLENCE THROUGH STUDY
LIVERPOOL	haec otia studia fovent	THESE LEISURE DAYS FOSTER LEARNING
MANCHESTER	cognitio sapientia humanitas	KNOWLEDGE, WISDOM, HUMANITY
NAPIER	nisi sapientia frustra	FRUSTRATION WITHOUT WISDOM
NOTTINGHAM	sapientia urbs conditur	A CITY IS FOUNDED ON WISDOM
OXFORD	dominus illuminatio mea	THE LORD IS MY LIGHT (PSALMS)
SALFORD	altiora petamus	LET US SEEK HIGHER THINGS
SHEFFIELD/LSE	rerum cognoscere causas	TO DISCOVER THE CAUSES OF THINGS (VIRGIL)
WARWICK	mens agitat molem	THE MIND MOVES MATTER (VIRGIL)
YORK	in limine sapientiae	ON THE THRESHOLD OF WISDOM
Cambridge Colleges		
DOWNING	quaerere verum	SEEK THE TRUTH
FITZWILLIAM	ex antiquis et novissimis optima	BEST OUT OF OLD AND NEW
HOMERTON	respice finem	LOOK TO THE END
KING'S COLLEGE	veritas et utilitas	TRUTH AND USEFULNESS
QUEEN'S	floreat domus	MAY THIS HOUSE FLOURISH
TRINITY	virtus vera nobilitas	VIRTUE IS THE TRUE NOBILITY
Oxford Colleges		
WOLFSON	hunami nil alienum	NOTHING ALIEN TO ME AS A HUMAN (TERENCE)

UNIVERSITY	MOTTO	TRANSLATION
London Colleges IMPERIAL	*scientia imperii decus et tutamen*	KNOWLEDGE IS THE ADORNMENT AND PROTECTION OF THE EMPIRE
KING'S	*sancte et sapienter*	WITH HOLINESS AND WISDOM
LONDON SCHOOL OF ECONOMICS	*coniunctis viribus*	WITH UNITED POWERS
QUEEN MARY UNIVERSITY	*cuncti adsint meritaeque expectent praemia palmae*	LET ALL BE PRESENT AND LET THEM AWAIT THE REWARDS OF A DESERVED PRIZE (VIRGIL)

ROMAN HOLIDAY

There are many Roman sites to visit in continental Europe and further afield, some of which have been designated World Heritage Sites and others which have yet to be discovered by mass tourism. Bridges, aqueducts, palaces, villas, forums, temples, theatres, amphitheatres, whole towns and museums await the adventurous – while some are very well known, others are surprisingly overlooked. Here are a few suggestions...

COUNTRY	ROMAN SITE
ALBANIA	BUTRINT
ALGERIA	TIPASA
AUSTRIA	CARNUNTUM, FLAVIA SOLVA
BELGIUM	TONGEREN
BULGARIA	SOZOPOL
CROATIA	PULA, SPLIT
CYPRUS	SALAMIS
EGYPT	ALEXANDRIA
FRANCE	GLANUM (ST RÉMY), GRAND, PONT DU GARD, NIMES, ARLES, LYON, FRÉJUS, ORANGE, NICE-CIMIEZ
GERMANY	HECHINGEN-STEIN VILLA, REGENSBURG, SAALBURG, WALDGIRMES
GREECE	CORINTH, OLYMPIA, NICOPOLIS
ISRAEL	MASADA
ITALY	ROME, POMPEII, HERCULANEUM, CAPRI, LUNA, FIESOLE
JORDAN	JERASH
LEBANON	BAALBEK, BYBLOS, TYRE
LIBYA	LEPTIS MAGNA, SABRATHA, CYRENE
MOROCCO	VOLUBILIS
PORTUGAL	EVORA, CONIMBRIGA
ROMANIA	TROPAEUM TRAIANI
SPAIN	NUMANTIA, SEGOVIA, MERIDA, TARRAGONA, SAGUNTO
SWITZERLAND	VINDONISSA, MARTIGNY, AVENTICUM. AUGUSTA RAUONRICA
SYRIA	PALMYRA, LATAKIA
TUNISIA	CARTHAGE, DOUGGA, EL DJEM
TURKEY	MILETUS, MYRA, EPHESUS, PERGAMUM, DIDYMA, APHRODISIAS, PERGE
USA	LAS VEGAS NV (CAESAR'S PALACE FOR THE FAKE), MALIBU CA (J. PAUL GETTY MUSEUM FOR THE REAL STUFF)

LAW

Lawyers' Latin by John Gray provides a comprehensive cover but here are some of the more familiar legal phrases, which are unlikely to die out immediately despite recent attempts to discourage their use. These then are the 'remnants of a residue' as Nicholas Ostler elegantly puts it in his *Ad Infinitum*.

LATIN	TRANSLATION
actus reus	GUILTY ACT (THE CHARGE AGAINST THE ACCUSED)
ad colligenda bona	TO COLLECT THE GOODS [OF THE DECEASED]
ad hoc	TO THIS [PURPOSE] (DECISION TO BE MADE DEPENDING ON THE SITUATION)
ad idem	TO THE SAME [OPINION] (BOTH PARTIES AGREE ON THIS POINT)
ad infinitum	TO INFINITE (CONTINUING WITHOUT END)
ad litem	FOR THE LAWSUIT (USED OF TEMPORARY APPOINTMENTS)
amicus Curiae	A FRIEND OF THE COURT (A NEUTRAL VIEWPOINT)
bona fide	IN GOOD FAITH (WITHOUT THE INTENTION OF FRAUD)
bona vacantia	VACANT GOODS (NO ONE ENTITLED TO AN ESTATE SO THE CROWN GETS IT)
compos mentis	COMPOSED OF MIND (I.E. SANE), OFTEN USED IN THE NEGATIVE *noncompos mentis*
cor / coram	IN THE PRESENCE OF
corpus delicti	BODY OF CRIME (THE BODY HERE BEING EVIDENCE)
de bonis non administratis	CONCERNING GOODS NOT ADMINISTERED (REFERRING TO DIVISIONS YET TO BE MADE BY A SECOND ADMINISTRATOR)
de iure	BY RIGHT

LATIN MATTERS

LATIN	TRANSLATION
doli incapax	INCAPABLE OF CRIME
duces tecum	YOU WILL BRING WITH YOU (A DOCUMENT TO COURT)
ex gratia	OUT OF A GRACE (AN AWARD MADE WITHOUT ACCEPT-ANCE OF BLAME)
ex officio	OUT OF DUTY (WHERE A HOLDER OF ONE OFFICE IS ENTI-TLED TO HOLD ANOTHER)
ex parte	BY A PARTY (WHEN THE OTHER PARTY ISN'T PRESENT OR NOTIFIED)
ex post facto	BY A SUBSEQUENT ACT (DONE AFTER BUT HAS A RETRO-SPECTIVE EFFECT)
forum conveniens	AT AN APPROPRIATE PLACE (OFTEN USED IN NEGATIVE *forum non conveniens* WHERE A COURT CAN SUGGEST A MORE CONVENIENT FORUM)
functus officio	ONE HAVING PERFORMED DUTY (SO NO MORE CAN BE DONE BY THAT PERSON)
habeas corpus	[A DEMAND THAT] YOU HAVE THE BODY (WRIT TO A CUS-TODIAN TO PRODUCE PRISONER BEFORE COURT TO JUDGE LEGALITY OF DETENTION)
ignorantia iuris non excusat	IGNORANCE OF THE LAW IS NO EXCUSE (AN UNPERMITTED DEFENCE)
in camera	IN THE CHAMBER (A PRIVATE HEARING)
in Curia	IN OPEN COURT (A PUBLIC HEARING)
in flagrante delicto	IN THE BLAZING ACT (CAUGHT RED-HANDED)
in loco parentis	IN THE PLACE OF A PARENT (RESPONSIBILITY TO ACT AS A PARENT)
in personam	AGAINST THE PERSON (AN ACTION AGAINST AN INDIVID-UAL)
in rem	AGAINST THE MATTER (AN ACTION DIRECTED AGAINST PROPERTY OR STATUS ON A NON-SPECIFIED PERSON)
in situ	IN ITS [ORIGINAL] SITUATION
intra vires	WITHIN THE POWER [OF THE COURT]
ipsissima verba	THE VERY WORDS
ipso facto	BY THAT VERY FACT (BEST UNDERSTOOD IN THE EXAMPLE, A BLIND PERSON, *ipso facto*, CANNOT HOLD A DRIVING

LATIN	TRANSLATION
	LICENCE)
locus in quo	THE PLACE IN WHICH (SCENE OF THE EVENT)
mens rea	GUILTY MIND (THE CRIMINAL INTENTION)
mutatis mutandis	WITH THE NECESSARY CHANGES [AMENDMENTS] HAVING BEEN MADE
nulla bona	NO ASSETS (WHICH CAN BE SEIZED FROM A GUILTY DEFENDANT)
obiter dictum	SOMETHING SAID IN PASSING (BY A JUDGE AND NOT CONSTITUTING EVIDENCE OR JUDGEMENT)
per se	BY ITSELF
prima facie	AT FIRST SIGHT (SUFFICIENT EVIDENCE, UNLESS DISPROVED, TO PROVE A CASE)
pro bono (publico)	FOR THE (PUBLIC) GOOD (USED OF VOLUNTARY WORK)
pro forma	AS A MATTER OF FORM (FACILITATES LEGAL PROCEDURES)
pro tem / pro tempore	FOR THE TIME BEING
quasi	AS IF (NOT EXACTLY WHAT IT MIGHT APPEAR)
ratio decidendi	THE REASON FOR DECISION (USED BY COURT, USUALLY BOUND BY PRINCIPLES OF LAW)
res iudicata	A THING ADJUDGED (FINAL DECISION ON A CASE WHICH CANNOT BE RE-RAISED)
res ipsa loquitur	THE VERY THING SPEAKS FOR ITSELF (PROOF OF THE CASE IS SELF-EVIDENT)
sine die	WITHOUT A DAY (AN ADJOURNMENT WITH A RECONVENING DATE HELD OPEN)
sine qua non	WITHOUT WHICH [IT CAN] NOT [BE] (I.E. AN ESSENTIAL INGREDIENT)
sub iudice	UNDER JUDGEMENT (DETAILS OF PROCEEDINGS CANNOT BE DISCLOSED)
subpoena	UNDER A PENALTY (A WRIT DIRECTED TO A WITNESS TO APPEAR AT COURT)
ultra vires (nihil aggregiendum)	(NOTHING SHOULD BE TAKEN ON) BEYOND THE POWER (OF THE COURT'S JURISDICTION)

TEXT ABBREVIATIONS AND WORDS

Many written works contain Latin phrases and words, often abbreviated.

Here are some in current use:

ABBREVIA-TION	IN FULL	MEANING
A.D.	(anno domino)	IN THE YEAR OF OUR LORD
A.M.	(ante meridiem)	BEFORE MIDDAY
ANTE	-	BEFORE (INDICATING AN EARLIER PASSAGE)
C./CA.	(circa)	ABOUT/APPROXIMATELY
CF.	(confer)	COMPARE
CP.	(compara)	COMPARE
E.G.	(exempli gratia)	FOR THE SAKE OF AN EXAMPLE (A RELEVANT EXAMPLE TO QUALIFY A STATEMENT)
ET AL.	(et alii/alia)	AND OTHER PEOPLE/THINGS
ETC.	(et cetera)	AND THE REMAINING THINGS
FL.	(floruit)	HE/SHE/IT FLOURISHED (WHEN A PERSON WAS ACTIVE)
IBID.	(ibidem)	IN THE SAME PLACE (PREVIOUSLY MENTIONED)
ID./EAD.	(idem/eadem)	THE SAME MAN/WOMAN
I.A.	(inter alia)	AMONG OTHER THINGS
I.E.	(id est)	THAT IS (EXPLAINS A STATEMENT)
N.B.	(nota bene)	NOTE WELL (PARTICULARLY)
P.A.	(per annum)	THROUGH A YEAR (ANNUALLY)
P.M.	(post meridiem)	AFTER MIDDAY
P.P.	(per procurationem)	THROUGH ANOTHER (DELEGATE) ON BEHALF OF SOMEONE

ABBREVIATIONS

ABBREVIA-TION	IN FULL	MEANING
P.S.	*(post scriptum)*	AFTER WHAT'S WRITTEN (AN ADDITION)
Q.E.D.	*(quod erat demonstrandum)*	WHAT WAS TO BE PROVED [HAS BEEN]
Q.V.	*(quod vide)*	WHICH SEE (LOOK UP ELSEWHERE IN CURRENT TEXT)
POST	-	AFTER (INDICATING A LATER PASSAGE)
PRO RATA		IN PROPORTION
RE	*(in re)*	IN THE MATTER OF/CONCERNING (NOW REBORN IN EMAILS)
SC.	*(scilicet / scire licet)*	IT IS PERMITTED TO KNOW/THAT'S TO SAY (LESS USED THAN I.E.)
SIC	-	THUS (BUT MAY BE WRONG)
STET	-	LET IT STAND (DON'T CHANGE)
V.I.	*(vide infra)*	SEE BELOW
V.I.	*(vide supra)*	SEE ABOVE
VIZ	*(videlicet / videre licet)*	IT IS PERMITTED TO SEE/NAMELY (INDICATES EXAMPLES)
V./VS	*(versus)*	AGAINST

A little bit of latin...

Far out, man

Where did Procul Harum's manager learn Latin? If he wanted 'beyond these things', it should be *'ultra has.'*

    procul harum means something like 'far of all these things.' But like their puzzling 1967 hit 'A Whiter Shade of Pale', it sure sounds good though.

QUIZ III: FILM HITS

IDENTIFY THE CINEMATIC HITS

All the movies in this quiz made an impact at the box office and are all well known. The accepted release year (or years in the case of identically titled remakes) follow.

Giveaway parts of titles such as *Harry Potter, Indiana Jones, Lord of the Rings* and *Pirates of the Caribbean* have been dropped, just to make it a little trickier. Titles with an exclamation mark are taking a real liberty!

For example I could have written *quiritatio sine oculo* meaning 'shriek without an eye', or even *quitiratio sine ego* meaning 'shriek without 'I' in really bad Latin to get to *Shrek* (and even then there's the false alarm of *Scream*, hence the year to avoid confusion) but I wouldn't be that mean. Or would I?

The Early Years of Cinema

Albus Niveus cum septem pumilionibus (1937); *egressus vento* (1939); *casa alba* (1942); *femina scelesta* (1946/1980); *ter-*

tius vir (1949); *caerulea lucerna* (1950); *bellum mundorum* (1953/2005); *medicus adest* (1954); *et ego et rex* (1956); *decem imperia* (1956); *circum orbem terrarum octoginta diebus* (1956/2004); *dormiens pulchra puella* (1959)

The Sixties and Seventies

Maris undecim (1960/2001); *superbi septem* (1960); *centum et uni canes* (1961/1996); *iuvenes* (1961); *trecenti [Lacedaemonii]* (1962/2006); *longissima dies* (1962); *mea pulchra femina* (1964); *iuva!* (1965); *sonitus carminum* (1965); *ubi aquilae audent* (1968); *o, iecur!* (1968); *proelium Britanniae* (1969); *fabula amoris* (1970); *vir qui obtulit aliquid quod non recusandum erat* (1972); *sellae equitationis incandescentes* (1974); *turris ignis* (1974); *dentes maris* (1975); *bella stellarum: spes nova* (1977) *pons plus* (1977); *ea quae non nata est in terra* (1979)

The Eighties and Nineties

imperium repugnat (1980); *currus ignis* (1981); *id quod non natum est in terra* (1982); *templum mortis* (1984); *redite ad futurum* (1985); *ex Africa* (1985); *optima hasta (!)* (1986); *improba saltatio* (1987); *ultimum iter pro bono* (1989); *vir qui est similis mammali noctis* (1989); *umbra* (1990); *domi solus* (1990); *femina pulchra* (1990); *silentium agnorum* (1991); *hortus antiquorum animalium* (1993); *quattuor nuptiae funusque unum* (1993); *leo regius* (1994); *Romanus deus solis, tredecim* (1995); *maxima navis quae summersa est* (1997); *viri in vestibus nigris* (1997); *tres viri infansque* (1997); *scriptor notus in amore* (1998); *mater* (!) (1999); *non in colle* (!) (1999); *sextus sensus* (1999)

The Noughties

illud quod subiacet (2000); *illa quae feminae cupiunt* (2000); *conveniamus parentes* (2000); *tempestas optima* (2000); *cubiculum celatarum rerum* (2002); *signa* (2002); *de puero* (2002); *heros araneus* (2002); *rex redit* (2003); *inveniens 'no-one'* (2003); *amor re vera* (2003); *arca mortui* (2006); *laeti pedes* (2006); *ludi senioris carmina* (2006); *expiatio* (2007); *nulla patria senibus* (2007); *erit sanguis* (2007)

MEDICINE

There is a tremendous amount of Latin in the field of medicine, a hangover from the time when all scientific documents were written in Latin to gain the widest possible circulation.

In bones alone one will find *tibia, fibula* (brooch), *femur, ulna, radius, humerus* (funny bone), *patella* (little plate), *scapula, pelvis* (basin), *carpus, costa, os calcis* (bone of the heel) and *vertebrae*.

Muscles are *flexores, extensores, levatores* and *rotatores* according to function, e.g. *flexores digitorum, extensor pollicis*.

The principal vein is the *superior vena cava*.

Latin abbreviations for prescriptions provide a good code, but if one can read the doctor's writing, it can be cracked.

On the subject of body parts, the Romans had great fun with the names of the various fingers (*digiti*) of the hand. The *pollex* is the thumb (and big toe), the *index* does the pointing, the middle finger is, somewhat neutrally, the *medius* (or more controversially the *infamis* for time-honoured rude gesticulations!), the *anularius* wore a ring (anulus) and the little one is the *auricularius*, judged most suitable for cleaning out the ear wax of one's *auris*.

Abbreviation	Latin	Meaning
AD.	*adde*	ADD
AD LIB.	*ad libitum*	AT WILL
AQ.	*aqua*	WATER
B.I.D./B.D.	*bis in die*	TWICE DAILY
C.	*cum*	WITH
D. IN P. AEQ.	*divide in partes aequales*	DIVIDE EQUALLY
F./FT.	*fiat*	LET THERE BE MADE, I.E. MAKE
F.H.	*fiat haustus*	MAKE A DRINK
F.M.	*fiat mistura*	MAKE A MIXTURE
F.PIL.	*fiat pillula*	MAKE A PILL
GTT./GUTT.	*gutta*	A DROP
N.P.O.	*nil per os*	NIL BY MOUTH
O.N.	*omni nocte*	NIGHTLY
Q.S.	*quantum sufficit*	AS MUCH AS NECESSARY
R.	*recipe*	TAKE
T.I.D./T.D.	*ter in die*	THRICE DAILY

CHEMICAL SYMBOLS

Many chemical symbols were named from the Greek places and people but there are also ones with Latin origins – thus explaining some of the seemingly bizarre symbols. Not all of the following were known to the Romans.

Symbol	Origin	Meaning	Element
Ag	argentum	SILVER, MONEY	SILVER
Al	alumen	ALUM	ALUMINIUM
Au	aurum	GOLD, SHINING DAWN	GOLD
C	carbo	CHARCOAL	CARBON
Ca	calx	LIME, CHALK	CALCIUM
Cs	caesius	SKY-BLUE, GREY-BLUE	CAESIUM
Cu	cuprum	CYPRUS METAL	COPPER
Fe	ferrum	IRON, SWORD	IRON
Ga	Gallia	GAUL *	GALLIUM
Hg	Hydrargyrum [Latinised Greek]	-	MERCURY
Ir	iris	RAINBOW	IRIDIUM
K	kallium [new Latin]	-	POTASSIUM
Mg	magnes	MAGNET	MANGANESE
N	nitrum	NATIVE SODA	NITROGEN
Na	natrium [new Latin]	-	SODIUM
Pb	plumbum	LEAD, PIPE	LEAD
Ra	Rhenus	RAY	RADIUM
Re	Ruthenia	RHINE	RHENIUM
Ru	Scandia	RUSSIA	RUTHENIUM
Sc	silex	SCANDINAVIA	SCANDIUM
Si	stannum	FLINT	SILICON
Sn	stibium	TIN	TIN
Sb	sulphur	ANTIMONY	ANTIMONY
S	tellus	SULPHUR, BRIMSTONE	SULPHUREARTH
Te		EARTH	TELLURIUM

*The discoverer was a Frenchman, a Gaul, called Lecocq (the rooster) and the Latin for rooster is *gallus*. So rather witty.

CLASSIFICATION

A big hooray for the Swede Carolus Linnaeus for not only having a very Romanesque name but also for establishing Latin, along with, to a certain extent, Greek, as the language of botany in the 18th century. His nomenclature in *Systema Naturae* describes the whole of nature as he knew it into the hierarchy of kingdoms, classes, orders, genera, species and varieties. Genus (e.g. *canis*) and species (e.g. *familiaris*) are the familiar make-up of a scientific name to form a library of hundreds of thousands.

Some of them are quite amusing as Richard Fortey points out in *Dry Store Room No. 1* who laments that the mollusc *abra* lost its species *cadabra*. Duly revised it was reassigned to a new genus to make the less memorable *theora cadabra*. But there's still *agra phobia, agra vation, apopyllus now, dissup irae, eubetia bigaulae* (say aloud in English pronunciation), *ittibittium, kamera lens, pieza rhea, ptomaspis dikenaspis ariaspis* (remove the aspis), *verae peculya, arses, silybum*.

One may suspect that our eminent scientists are not taking nomenclature as seriously as they ought, while Latin names are abandoned for some entertaining puns. Not that Latin is devoid of it, of course, viz a recently extinct parrot called *vini vidivici* and the water beetle *Ytu Brutus*.

Here is a selection of some common Latin names found in British life, many taken from Paul Sterry's *Complete British Wildlife*.

Mammals

canis familiaris	domestic dog
canis lupus	wolf
felis catus	domestic cat
felis sylvestris	wild cat
glis glis	edible dormouse
homo sapiens	man
lutra lutra	otter
meles meles	badger
mus musculus	house mouse
mustela erminea	stoat
rattus norvegicus	brown rat
sciuris carolinensis	grey squirrel
sciuris vulgaris	red squirrel
vulpes vulpes	fox

Birds

corvus corax	raven
cuculus canorus	cuckoo
passer domesticus	house sparrow
picus viridis	green woodpecker
riparia riparia	sand martin
troglodytes troglodytes	wren
turdus merula	blackbird
turdus musicus	song thrush

Reptiles

natrix natrix	grass snake

Amphibians

bufo bufo	common toad
rana temporaria	common frog

Fish

anguilla anguilla	eel
salmo trutta	trout

Insects

apis mellifera	honeybee
lasius niger	black garden ant
musca domestica	common house-fly
vespula vulgaris	common wasp

Trees and Shrubs

acer pseudoplatanus	sycamore
aesculus	
hippocastanum	horse-chestnut
hedera helix	ivy
ilex aquifolium	holly
quercus robur	English oak
taxus baccata	yew

Fruit

citrus sinensis	orange
fragaria species	strawberry
malus pumila	apple
musa sapientum	banana
pyrus communis	pear
vitis vinifera	grape

Vegetables

allium cepa	onion
allium porrum	leek
allium sativum	garlic
brassica oleracea capitata	cabbage
brassica oleracea gemmifera	Brussels sprout
brassica oleracea italica	broccoli
brassica rapa	watercress
daucus carota	carrot
pisium sativum	pea
solanum tuberosum	potato
spinacia oleracea	spinach

RUDE LATIN

This is the naughty section for the intellectually curious as well as those who perhaps enjoy tormenting their Latin schoolmasters with inquiries such as, 'Sir, what's the Latin for six tall pine trees?' The answer is of course *sex erecti pinus*. Cue tittering.

So perhaps that's a good place to start.

A penis is of course *penis*, originally a tail but a meaning soon lost to accepted scientific appellation, but more obscene are *mentula*, matching the female *cunnus*. Catullus used this as a nickname. If erect or exposed by circumcision *verpa* was preferred and Catullus uses the adjective *verpus*. Catullus also mentions *sopio* which was an enormous Priapic caricature depicted in paintings such as in the House of the Vettii in Pompeii as well as appearing in graffiti there. Martial mentions the childish-sounding *pipinna*, 'thingy', and of course there is much potential for synonyms as the Latin for mast, flagpole etc … you get the idea.

coleus ('cojones' is a popular word in Spanish) and

testis are words for a testicle, the latter interesting in that one 'testified' in court by holding one's precious possessions. Cicero discusses these words among many other potential rude words in his *epistulae ad familiares*.

The female *pudenda* (originally 'shameful' in Latin) is *cunnus*, later *cunna* in a change of gender, quite an obscene word according to Cicero who explains the curiosity of why Latin prefers *nobiscum* to *cum nobis* to mean 'with us', namely to avoid the ablative of *cunnus*. Horace blames Helen of Troy's 'bits' as the cause of the Trojan War. Sometimes the innocent *sinus* (fold) and *fossa* (ditch) could become synonyms. *vagina* originally meant scabbard. Catullus and Martial mention *cunnilingus*, used unchanged today. *landica*, the clitoris, is evidently seriously forbidden as Cicero refuses to write it out, instead cleverly coming close with *illam dicam* (I may say that thing) but it appears in Pompeiian graffiti.

clunis, *culus* (very popular as 'culo' in Italian and Spanish) and *anus* (ring) are colourful words for the bottom. Unchanged *merda* is as popular in Italian as it was in Martial's day though a politer, at least it appears in the Psalms, form of manure emerged as *stercus*. To produce said manure, the verb *cacare* (to defecate) has spread to

German, Dutch and Russian as well as enjoying its customary Romantic lineage.

Horace mentions *pedere* (to fart) in his *sermones* and this word is the origin of the intriguing phrase 'hoist with one's own petard', as quoted in *Hamlet*, but not so curious when one realises a petard was a bomb. *mingere* is simply to have a pee while *meiere* can have connotations of ejaculation. The product of the former is *urina* or *lotium*, the latter related to *lavare* (to wash) because the Romans used the ammonia of urine for their laundry.

futuere (to copulate), today's most popular four-letter word, was equally a hit with Martial, Catullus and Pompeiian graffiti artists, a personal favourite being the female's stark effort, *fututa sum hic* (I got a good shagging here). It seems that there were stronger words to match the aggression of today's favourite Anglo-Saxon monosyllabic utterance such as Catullus' *pedicabo* (literally 'I shall practice unnatural vice') and *irrumabo* (literally 'I shall treat obscenely'). Less graphic is the gentle *coire* (to go with) as in the current use of *coitus* in English, while Martial came up with some variations using *cevere* for a male receiving male sex and *crisare* for a female receiving a male.

LATIN WORDS IN ENGLISH

Not spoken, hey? Any of these words ring a bell?

abacus abdomen aborigines actor acumen addendum administrator agenda aggressor agitator album alias alibi altar alumnus amen animal animus annotator ante antenna anterior apex apparatus appendix aquarium area arena aroma asparagus assessor asylum auditorium aura axis basis benefactor biceps bonus cactus cadaver calculator camera campus caper captor caret caveat censor census cinnamon circus citrus clamour climax coitus collector colon colossus coma comma commentator compendium competitor compressor conductor consensus consortium continuum contractor cornucopia corpus cranium crater creator creditor credo crisis crux curator data decorum deficit delirium demonstrator dictator dictum dilemma diploma discus distributor doctor dogma drama duo duplicator echo editor educator ego elevator emphasis emporium enema enigma error exit exterior exterminator extra facile factor fiat focus formula forum fungus furore gemini genesis genius geranium gladiator gusto gymnasium habitat hiatus horizon horror hyena hyphen icon idea ignoramus illustrator imitator impostor impromptu incubator index indicator inertia inferior inquisitor insomnia inspector instigator instructor interest interim interior interrogator investigator iris item janitor junior languor legislator lens liberator liquor major mania martyr matrix mausoleum maximum mediator medium mentor minimum minister minor minus miser moderator momentum monitor moratorium motor murmur museum narrator nausea navigator nectar neuter nucleus oasis objector ode omen onus opera operator opus orator osmosis pallor panacea par paralysis pastor patina pauper pelvis peninsula perpetrator persecutor persona petroleum phoenix phosphorus plasma platinum plus podium pollen possessor posterior prior professor progenitor propaganda prosecutor prospectus protector quantum quota rabies radius ratio receptor recipe rector referendum regalia regimen renovator rostrum saliva sanatorium scintilla sculptor sector senator senior series serum simile sinister siren solarium species specimen spectator spectrum sponsor stadium status stigma stimulus stratum stupor successor superior tandem tenor terminus terror torpor transgressor translator tremor tribunal trio trivia tuba tutor ulterior vacuum verbatim vector vertigo vesper veto victor vigil villa virus visa vortex **and many more.**

ROMAN SITES TO VISIT IN BRITAIN

There are hundreds of Roman sites in England so the following list will just have to be a selection of greatest hits. Many are run by English Heritage or the National Trust.

A good day out beckons.

Fishbourne

At Fishbourne on the Sussex coast, workmen digging a ditch in 1960 discovered Roman remains. Archaeologists proceeded to excavate over half of a sizeable palace. The north wing is uncovered and roofed over and open as a museum. Here one can see various archaeological treasures, like mosaic floors with hypocaust heating underneath, a skeleton, a boy's mask, a small ring suggesting that children lived there and charred door sills suggesting that there had once been a fire. In fact the fire destroyed the palace and after being looted it was forgotten for over 1,000 years. An inscription dedicated to Neptune and Minerva was discovered in the nearby city of Chichester, known in Roman times as *Noviomagus*. It was dedicated by Cogidubnus, or possibly Togidubnus, king of the Regnenses, a British tribe. It is thought that the palace was given to him as a reward for his help given to Emperor Claudius' invading army in 43 AD.

Hadrian's Wall

Adopted by his predecessor Traianus or Trajan, Publius Hadrianus was emperor from 117 to 138 AD. He called a halt to Trajan's policy of expanding the empire and chose instead to consolidate the defences in Britain, Germany and Numidia. Britain's wall was built to keep out the marauding tribes of the north. Its remains have survived well, running from Newcastle to Carlisle. Three legions built the wall between 122 and 129 AD. Incorporated into the wall were sixteen forts, large enough to house a thousand men, seventy-nine towers known as milecastles and, between each milecastle, two turrets for use as lookout posts. The most famous sites of the wall are Housesteads and *Vindolanda*, both halfway along the wall and within spitting distance of each other. Later a further wall was added further north, known as the Antonine Wall.

Aquae Sulis

The waters of the goddess Sulis or Minerva with whom the Romans equated her were Roman baths established in about 80 AD and used for over 300 years. They were found in Bath in 1775 and now are one of the most spectacular Roman sites in England. Highlights include a giant stone Medusa's head and a bronze head of Minerva herself.

Bignor Roman villa

Bignor is close to Arundel in West Sussex and in its Roman heyday boasted seventy buildings and over forty acres. The villa was discovered in 1811. The museum contains an impressive array of mosaics and the winter *triclinium* has the celebrated 'Venus and the Gladiators'.

Chedworth Roman villa

Discovered in 1864, a couple of baths and more mosaics can be viewed at Yanworth near Cheltenham, Gloucestershire.

Lullingstone Roman villa

This villa was discovered as recently as 1939 and exca-vated from 1949 and can be found in Eynsford, Kent.

The *triclinium* mosaic is mythological depicting separately Europa and Bellerophon.

Wall
This is on the important Roman road of Watling Street which starts at London's Edgware Road. It was an army post containing the *Letocetum* baths and is at Wall near Lichfield in Staffordshire.

Wroxeter
This was the old Roman city of *Viroconium*, found east of Shrewsbury in Shropshire. It boasts a bath and forum.

Inchtuthil
This was a short-lived Roman fortress near Perth, possibly housing the XX Legion who left in an awful hurry, abandoning a valuable seven tons of iron nails.

Dorchester
The Romans built this town *Durnovaria* as a capital for the Durotriges tribe to replace the Iron-Age Maiden Castle, scene of fierce fighting, close by.

London

There is little left of *Londinium* after bombing and rebuilding though one can see the Temple of Mithras on Queen Victoria Street EC4 and an amphitheatre under Guildhall Yard. The Museum of London has a major Roman collection.

York

Eboracum was a major town there are remains of wall and excavations of a baths, a temple and cemeteries outside the city wall. The Yorkshire Museum contains many Roman archaeological finds. To the northeast on the North Yorkshire Moors is the Roman road on Wheeldale Moor.

St Albans

Verulamium is famous for its preservation of a rare Roman theatre and was clearly an important centre.

Caerleon

Isca in South Wales has a massive legionary fortress, home to the II Legion Augusta, together with a fine amphitheatre.

Richborough

Rutupiae in Kent is thought to be the spearhead of the
Roman invasion in 43AD, now two miles in from the
coast. There is an amphitheatre, a fort and the remains
of a mighty triumphal arch.

THE ROMAN MYSTERIES

The Roman Mysteries are a series of seventeen history
mystery novels for children, but very satisfying for adults,
impeccably researched and written by Caroline Lawrence.
Set from 79 AD (the eruption of Mount Vesuvius) onwards,
they present a splendid take on Roman life, examining
Roman mores as well as weaving in Greek myths, and
frequently branch out from Ostia where the four young
protagonists live. The BBC filmed the series in 2006 and
2007. Copies, signed by Caroline, receive the following
Latin tagd taken from, or inspired by, the story.

I *Thieves of Ostia: cave canem*
The well-known mosaic found in the House of the
Tragic Poet in Pompei.

II *Secrets of Vesuvius: fortes fortuna iuvat*
'Fortune favours the brave', first used by Terence but
nicked by Virgil as *audentes fortuna iuvat* in his Aeneid.

III *Pirates of Pompeii: volare*
volare, cantare (Italian but matching the Latin perfectly)
comes from a 1958 Italian eurovision song and has been
covered many times, the best-known version perhaps
being Dean Martin's.

IV *Assassins of Rome: lacrimae rerum*
sunt lacrimae rerum et mentem mortalia tangunt is from
Virgil's Aeneid I. 'There are tears of things and mortal
deeds touch the heart', weeps Aeneas as he remembers
his fallen Trojan comrades.

V *Dolphins of Laurentum: morbo medeor*
novum vetus vinum bibo novo veteri morbo medeor.
As described by Varro this celebrates the vine harvest.

'I drink old and new wine, I am cured of old and new disease.'

VI *Twelve Tasks of Flavia Gemina: carpe diem*
carpe diem quam mininum credula postero is from Horace's Odes, addressed to Leuconoe. Seize, or pluck, the day, trusting tomorrow as little as possible.

VII *Enemies of Jupiter: ars longa*
ars longa vita brevis is from Hippocrates. 'Art lasts long but life is short.'

VIII *Gladiators from Capua: habet*
habet, hoc habet, cried by spectators as gladiatorial blows find their mark.

IX *Colossus of Rhodes: Hectora credas*
Si solum spectes caput, Hectora credas. si stantem videas Astyanacta putes. An epigram by Martial. 'If you saw only the head you'd think it was Hector, if you were to see him standing, Astyanax,' (who was Hector's son), i.e. Martial is talking about a dwarf.

X *Fugitive from Corinth:* γνωθι σεαυτον *(gnothi seauton)*
This one's Greek from the temple of Apollo in Delphi.

XI *Sirens of Surrentum:* *summum bonum*
The aim of Aristotle and followers to find the highest good.

XII *Charioteer of Delphi:* *naufragium*
'Shipwreck,' cry the spectators of the Circus Maximus when a chariot crashes, mangling driver and horses.

XIII *Slave-Girl from Jerusalem:* *vita brevis*
See VII.

XIV *Beggar of Volubilis:* *aliquid novi*
unde etiam vulgare Graeciae dictum semper aliquid novi Africam adferre is from Pliny's Natural History and translates, 'from where indeed [comes] the common saying of Greece that Africa always offers something new'.

XV *Scribes from Alexandria:* *tinea sum*
'I am a bookworm', the answer to a riddle attributed to Symposius;

Littera me pavit nec quid sit littera novi:
In libris vixi nec sum studiosior inde;
Exedi Musas nec adhuc tamen ipsa profeci.

I thrive on letters yet no letters I know.
I live in books: but no more studious so,
Though I devour the Muses, no wiser do I grow.

XVI Prophet from Ephesus: *diligamus invicem*
'Let us love one another', from the First Epistle of John
in the New Testament.

XVII Man from Pomegranate Street: *ne musca quidem*
'Not even a fly', as Domitian's secretary, Vibius Priscus,
would say to anyone asking if the emperor was busy
with anyone.

A little bit of latin...

U2 can listen
Bono, Paul Hewson of U2, owes his nickname to hearing aids
by *bonavox* (a good voice). After a gender change, since vox is
feminine, he became the *bono vox* of Dublin.

Quiz IV: Number One Pop Artists

Identify the following pop groups and solo artistes

All have reached No.1 in the UK singles chart between 1952 and 2008 at least once. As a hint, each act is listed under the year it first hit the top spot. These are, or were, all popular acts and artists. The Number One Hits section (on pages LVIII to LX), contains most of these as further clues.

Hint: Under 1955 could have come *pelvis sine piso preme partum* (!), i.e pelvis without a pea press meadow/lea so Elvis Presley. But that was a bit contorted, (hence the exclamation mark), and pelvis rather gave it away, anyway.

The *coleoptera*, or should that be the less mellifluous sounding *scarabei,* have been allotted their own section (see pages XVI to XVII).

porta est dies (!) (1954); *textores somniorum* (1956); *cicadae* (1957); *semper pratum fratres* (1958); *umbrae* (1961); *exquisitores* (1963); *animalia* and *saxa volventia* (both 1964); *fratres iusti, petitores, ilices aquifoliae, aves* and *apricus et divide* (!) (1965); *fratres qui ambulant, vultus parvi* and *pueri litoris* (all 1966); *simii qui litteras ordinare non possunt* (1967); *aurora, media via* and *necatus* (1971); *novi petitores* (1972); *decem vide vide* (!) (1973); *limus* and *tres adiunctivae quantitates* (1974); *regina* (1975) *hiems, ver, aestas, autumnus* and *res vera* (1976); *'lion' orator* and *alae* (1977); *vicani incolae* and *vigils* (1979); *primus vir et formicae* and *hominum foedus* (1981); *currisne? currisne?* (!) and *tu, age quadraginta* (1983); *stellarum navis* (1987); *madidus, umidus, udus* and *tu quoque* (1988); *novi iuvenes in via* and *animi stulti* (1989); *australis pulcher* (1990); *a pueris ad viros* (1992); *tene illud* (1993); *princeps* (1994); *arbores circum aquam in deserto* (1995); *puellae cibi acris* (1996); *totaliter beatae* (1998); *gradus* and *Britannum genu hastae* (1999); *dulces infantes* or perhaps *mellis bellissimae* (2002)

KEY HISTORICAL EVENTS IN ROMAN REPUBLICAN TIMES

Here are a few dates covering major Roman occurrences in the years BC (Before Christ) before Rome became an empire.

YEAR	EVENT
c. 1100 B.C.	THE LEGENDARY AENEAS ARRIVES IN ITALY FROM TROY.
753	LEGENDARY FOUNDATION OF ROME. 20TH APRIL.
750	ROMULUS DIRECTS THE RAPE OF THE SABINES.
c. 716	ROMULUS IS CARRIED UP TO HEAVENS. SUCCESSIVE KINGS ARE NUMA POMPILIUS, TULLUS HOSTILIUS, ANCUS MARTIUS, TARQUINIUS PRISCUS.
534	SERVIUS TULLIUS, 6TH KING, IS ASSASSINATED.
c. 510	TARQUINIUS SUPERBUS, 7TH KING, IS BANISHED BY NEPHEW BRUTUS WHO BECOMES ONE OF THE FIRST TWO CONSULS.
496	REGILLUS. ROME IS FORCED TO JOIN LATIN ALLIANCE V. AEQUI AND VOLSCI TRIBES.
450	12 TABLES ESTABLISHES LAW.
396	VEII, FURIUS CAMILLUS BEATS THE ETRUSCANS BUT IS EXILED.
387	ALLIA, GAULS BEAT ROMANS BUT MANLIUS AND GEESE SAVE THE CAPITOL. CAMILLUS IS RECALLED TO SEE OFF THE GAULS.

KEY HISTORICAL EVENTS IN ROMAN REPUBLICAN TIMES

YEAR	EVENT
370-336	PLEBEIANS PERMITTED TO STAND FOR THE CONSULSHIP, DICTATORSHIP AND PRAETORSHIP.
312	APPIUS CLAUDIUS BEGINS 132-MILE VIA APPIA LINKING ROME AND CAPUA.
295	SENTINUM, GAULS AND SAMNITES DEFEATED BY FABIUS AND DECIUS MUS.
280	PYRRHUS HIRED BY TARENTUM TO PREVENT ROMAN EXPANSION.
275	BENEVENTUM. AFTER 2 'PYRRHIC' VICTORIES, PYRRHUS IS DEFEATED.
264	DOMINATION OF ITALY COMPLETE.
264/241	1ST PUNIC WAR AGAINST THE CARTHAGINIANS IS FOUGHT OVER MESSANA.
218	HANNIBAL CROSSES THE ALPS WITH 35,000 MEN AND 37 ELEPHANTS STARTING THE 2ND PUNIC WAR.
217	LAKE TRASIMENE. HANNIBAL WINS WITH 25,000 MEN AND 1 ELEPHANT.
216	CANNAE, HANNIBAL DEFEATS FABIUS. MAHARBAL TELLS HIM, *vincere scis; victoria uti nescis.*
212	MARCELLUS CAPTURES SYRACUSE WHERE ARCHIMEDES IS KILLED.
202	ZAMA, SCIPIO 'AFRICANUS' DEFEATS HANNIBAL.
146	CARTHAGE IS DESTROYED ENDING 3RD PUNIC WAR. ROMANS CONTROL GREECE AFTER BATTLE OF CORINTH.
107	GAIUS MARIUS ALLOWS POOR TO JOIN THE ARMY.
82	SULLA DICTATOR FOR 3 YEARS.
73	SPARTACUS LEADS SLAVE REVOLT, SEIZING MOUNT VESUVIUS.
71	SPARTACUS IS DEFEATED BY CRASSUS AND POMPEY. 6,000 SLAVES HANGED ON THE APPIAN WAY.
70	CICERO PROSECUTES VERRES. CRASSUS AND POMPEY CONSULS.
67	POMPEY DEFEATS PIRATES.
63	CICERO, AS CONSUL, AVERTS CATILINE'S CONSPIRACY.
61	CLODIUS IS INVOLVED IN THE *Bona Dea* SCANDAL.

YEAR	EVENT
60	Caesar, Crassus, Pompey form 1st Triumvirate.
58	Cicero is banished for executing Catiline. Caesar campaigns in Gaul.
57	Milo secures Cicero's return.
55	Caesar visits Britain.
54	Caesar visits Britain again.
53	Carrhae, Crassus is killed by Parthians.
52	Gergovia + Alesia, Caesar fights Vercingetorix of the Gauls.
	Clodius is killed by Milo's men.
50	Civil war between Caesar and Pompey.
49	Caesar crosses the Rubicon (*alea iacta est*). Pompey and most of the senate flee.
48	Pompey is murdered by Ptolemy XII in Egypt after Pharsalia.
47	Zela (Syria). Caesar utters *veni, vidi, vici*.
46	Julian calendar realigns the year, with the year lasting 445 days.
45	Caesar adopts Octavius.
44	On the Ides (15 Mar.) Caesar is murdered by Cassius, Brutus and others in an attempt to preserve the republic.
43	Antonius, Octavianus, Lepidus form 2nd Triumvirate.
	Cicero is murdered by Antonius for speaking against him.
42	Philippi, Cassius and Brutus are defeated.
31	Actium, Antony and Cleopatra are defeated and commit suicide in 30.
27	Octavian becomes Augustus, thus bringing the republic to an end.

THE EMPERORS

Shortly before the birth of Jesus Christ the Roman republic collapsed and became an empire. For the next 100 years the emperors – well chronicled by writers such as Plutarch, Tacitus and Suetonius – provided a rich source of inspiration in modern popular culture – not only in cinematic epics but also on television – which examined the subject chronologically in *The Caesars* (1968) and *I Claudius* (1976), based on Robert Graves' *I Claudius* and sequel *Claudius the God*. Indeed this BBC production proves, over thirty years later, to contain the strongest portrayal with particularly Derek Jacobi making it impossible for anyone else to override his immediate identification with his role. *Anno Domini* (1985) and recently *Rome* (2005–7) have kept TV addicts well fuelled with the nefarious machinations of Roman emperors.

So here is a potted history of those emperors with a selection of their screen appearances.

AUGUSTUS (OCTAVIAN) (27 BC – 14 AD)

Gaius Octavius, born in 63 BC, was sensible enough to be adopted by Julius Caesar to become Gaius Julius Caesar Octavianus. He was an ally of Marcus Antonius (Mark Antony) when the two defeated Caesar's assassins Cassius and Brutus at Philippi, but the coalition was short-lived. Antony had become over-friendly with Cleopatra, the Greek queen of Egypt, whom Julius Caesar had also admired. Octavian defeated Antony in the naval battle of Actium in 31 BC after which Antony and Cleopatra committed suicide and he was able to obtain complete power. In 27 BC he changed his name to Augustus and became emperor (which Caesar never was) calling himself not emperor but *princeps* (first citizen) or *primus inter pares* (first among equals, a somewhat oxymoronic phrase much beloved over the ages and providing a title for Jeffrey Archer's novel). Augustus dramatically increased the *imperium Romanum* and protected his position by cutting down on the number of legions, increasing military service and establishing the Praetorian Guard. Poets Virgil and Horace, his contemporaries, were kind enough to immortalise his period of rule as the 'Golden Age' while Augustus blew his own trumpet with *res gestae*.

Augustus has been portrayed on the screen by Ian Keith in *Cleopatra* (1934), Bob Holt in *Julius Caesar* (1950), Douglas Watson in *Julius Caesar* (1953), most famously by Roddy McDowall in *Cleopatra* (1963), Richard Chamberlain in *Julius Caesar* (1970), John Castle in Antony and *Cleopatra* (1972) and Albert Lupo in *Son of Cleopatra* (1964). On TV, *The Caesars* and *I Claudius*, respectively Roland Culver and Brian Blessed.

TIBERIUS (14 – 37)

Tiberius became emperor after Augustus in 14 AD, but virtually retired to Capri in the Bay of Naples leaving Sejanus, an untrustworthy sidekick (who eventually had to be executed), to deal with the intrigues at Rome. The remains of his palace, called Villa Iovis, at Capri are situated at the top of a sheer cliff from where, it is said, much amusement was gained by pushing unfortunates over the edge.

Tiberius has been portrayed by Cedric Hardwicke in *Salome* (1953), Ernest Thesiger in *The Robe* (1953),

Hubert Rudley in *The Big Fisherman* (1959), George Relph in *Ben-Hur* (1959), Peter O'Toole in *Caligula* (1979) and Max von Sydow in *The Inquiry* (2006).

TV offered Andre Morell in *The Caesars*, George Baker in *I Claudius* and James Mason in AD.

CALIGULA (37 – 41)

Caligula, a nickname meaning 'little boot', was named Gaius and managed to rule for only four years. He seemed a pretty unspeakable fellow. For a really juicy account, read *I, Claudius* by Robert Graves. He received his just deserts by being murdered by the Praetorian Guard, theoretically the emperor's personal bodyguard, who then proclaimed Caligula's uncle Claudius emperor.

He was played by Emlyn Williams in *I Claudius* (1937), Jay Robinson in *The Robe* (1953) and again in its sequel *Demetrius and the Gladiators* (1954), and Malcolm McDowell in *Caligula* (1979) which spawned plenty of even more inferior imitations.

For television, Ralph Bates in *The Caesars*, John Hurt in *I Claudius*, John McEnery in AD.

CLAUDIUS (41 – 54)

Claudius engineered the invasion of Britain to exploit the gold, tin and iron there in 43 AD, brought rebellious king Caratacus to live in Rome as an exile in 51 AD, but married once too often and was poisoned by his fourth wife, Agrippina II, to secure the empire for her son of a previous marriage, Nero.

On screen: Charles Laughton in *I Claudius* (1937), Barry Jones in *Demetrius and the Gladiators* (1954), Peter Damon in *The Fall of the Roman Empire* (1964), Giancarlo Badessi in *Caligula* (1979), Jack Shepherd in *Boudica* (2003).

On television: Freddie Jones in *The Caesars*, stammering Derek Jacobi in *I, Claudius*.

NERO (54 – 68)

Nero succeeded Claudius thanks to his mother Agrippina's efforts. Rivals were quickly dispatched and calm rule was established under Seneca while Nero was young. Soon however Nero pursued the arts of singing and dancing much to the distaste of many. Boudica upset the peace in Britain in 61 AD and there were several plots against the emperor at Rome. In 64 AD a fire destroyed much of Rome; the Christians were blamed, though some thought Nero had started the fire so he could take the opportunity to build his dream golden palace, the *domus aurea*, remains of which can be seen near the Colosseum in Rome today. Nero killed his mother and two of his wives and suffered further revolts against him before he committed suicide with the immortal last words, '*qualis artifex pereo*' (what an artist the world is losing).

On screen: Charles Laughton in *The Sign of the Cross* (1932), twice by Gino Cervi in *Nerone e Messalina* (1949) and *OK Nerone* (1951), Peter Ustinov in *Quo Vadis* (1951) winning an Oscar, Peter Lorre in *The Story of Mankind* (1957), Patrick Cargill in *Up Pompeii* (1971), Dom DeLuise in *History of the World Part I* (1981), Andrew Lee Potts in *Boudica* (2003).

TV: Martin Potter in *The Caesars*, Christopher Biggins in *I Claudius*, Anthony Andrews in AD and Klaus Maria Brandauer in the miniseries *Quo Vadis?*

THE YEAR OF THE FOUR EMPERORS (68 – 69)

This year was marked by civil war. **Galba** didn't last long when the Praetorian Guard killed him. Successor Otho honourably committed suicide and **Vitellius** fell at the hands of Vespasian.

John Woodvine in *The Caesars* and Roy Purcell in *I, Claudius* have played Vitellius on TV. The names of Vitellius and Vespasian will also be familiar to the readers of Simon Scarrrow's *Eagle* novels.

VESPASIANUS (69 – 79)

An old soldier who had campaigned in Britain and Judaea (the latter a war which led to the sieges and falls of Jersualem in 70 and of Masada, along with mass suicide, in 73), Vespasian began the Colosseum and actually managed to die of natural causes and produced a famous deathbed quotation, *'vae, puto, deus fio'* – 'Woe (or should be whoa?), I think I'm turning into a god.' He also famously uttered, *'necesse est imperatori stanti mori'* – 'It's necessary for an emperor to die standing.'

Lindsey Davis set her Marcus Didius Falco novels during this reign.

TITUS (79 – 81)

Son of Vespasian, he coped with the eruption of Vesuvius in 79 AD, a fire at Rome and completed the Colosseum. He died probably of malaria and intriguingly said, 'I have made but one mistake.'

Caroline Lawrence set her series of *The Roman Mysteries* during this reign.

DOMITIANUS (81 – 96)

Domitian was the younger brother of Titus and given rather a bad press by contemporary writers. He was assassinated by the Praetorian Guard.

NERVA (96 – 98)

Nerva managed to live through Nero and his successors' reigns and was by now old and childless and thus not too much of a liability. He died of natural causes.

Norman Wooland remains the only screen Nerva in *Quo Vadis* (1951) though his predecessors are portrayed alongside earlier emperors, e.g. John Gielgud in *Caligula* (1979).

TRAIANUS (98 – 117)

Adopted son of Nerva, Trajan celebrated his victory over the Dacians with his famous column.

Amedeo Nazarri is the sole Trajan on screen in *Columna* (1968).

HADRIANUS (117 – 138)

Hadrian was widely considered a good egg, the third of the five so-called decent emperors and of course his wall still stands to a certain extent in north England. He died of natural causes.

ANTONINUS PIUS (138 – 161)

He was only pious in the sense that he encouraged Hadrian's deification and managed an impressively long reign. He also tried to build the Antonine Wall in Britain but it failed to have his predecessor's longevity. His last word was a password *'aequanimitas'* – equanimity.

MARCUS AURELIUS (161 – 180)

Things started to get complicated as Aurelius was co-emperor with Lucius Verus for a while and then again with his son Commodus, but this perhaps led to the collapse of the *pax Romana*. He was author of *meditationes*. Chickenpox killed him.

Alec Guinness played him in *The Fall of the Roman Empire* (1964), Richard Harris in *Gladiator* (2000).

COMMODUS (177 – 192)

Commodus' reign is considered the start of the end. He was particularly fond of naked personal gladiatorial combat, and so revolted many of his fellow Romans. He was strangled by a wrestler called Narcissus.

Both Christopher Plummer in *The Fall of the Roman Empire* (1964) and Joaquin Phoenix in *Gladiator* (2000) play Commodus as wonderfully deranged and they both suffer deaths in hand-to-hand combat.

From this age onwards, the Roman Empire decayed slowly with many of the emperors not particularly well-known (certainly Hollywood lost interest) to history and meeting violent deaths by being murdered or killed in battle as well as having easily muddled names like Constans, Constantius and Constantinus. And it was not helped by Diocletian's splitting of the empire between east and west in 284 AD.

CONSTANTINE (306 – 337)

Constantine stands apart from the later emperors for he was instrumental in ending the persecution of Christians in the empire after he defeated Maxentius in 312 at the battle of Milvian Bridge, where he is said to have received the divine '*in hoc signo, vinces*' – under the sign (of the cross), you will win. It didn't all go swimmingly for the Christians however, though later emperor Julian II admitted as he died in *363*, '*vicisti, Galilaee*'– you've won, man of Galilee – after failing to seize back the religious initiative.

Constantine held control of the Western Empire and

established a new capital at Byzantium, renaming it Constantinople in 330.

Constantine was portayed by Cornel Wilde in *Constantino il Grande* (1962) and by Robert Vincent Jones in *Nicholas of Myra* (2008)

Rome, capital of the western empire, suffered plundering by the Visigoths in 410, sacking by the Vandals in 455 and effectively ended after Romulus Augustus was forced to resign in 476, though the eastern empire survived for another millennium until the fall of Constantinople in 1453.

A little bit of latin...

Getting ink done

Latin lends *gravitas* to one's body artwork. Tattooists are inundated with requests for ink in Latin.

David Beckham has several tattoos, two of them in Latin; under his Manchester United number VII is *perfectio in spiritu* (perfection in spirit) and another *ut amem et foveam* (that I may love and cherish). The latter has a couple of lovely, golden even, present subjunctives.

Angelina Jolie's tattoo along her waist is *quod me nutrit me destruit* – what nourishes me destroys me.

Colin Farrell has used the old favourite *carpe diem*.

THE NUMBER ONE MOST FAMOUS ROMAN

JULIUS CAESAR

Born in 100 BC, Gaius Julius Caesar is the most famous of all Romans, thanks to his military achievements including his invasion of Britain or lack of it, his hair-style swept forward to cover recession, an affair with Queen Cleopatra of Egypt and a particularly dramatic death, made famous by Shakespeare, though instead of saying, '*et tu, Brute*', it is thought he said, 'καὶ σὺ, τέκνον'. He combined his expertise with the wealthy Crassus and the popular Pompey with whom he shared much power. He conquered Gaul between 58 and 51, but aroused the jealousy of many dangerous rivals in the senate at Rome. When Pompey joined in against him, Caesar crossed the River Rubicon, thereby declaring civil war and burning his bridges with the highly quotable, '*alea iacta est*'. After defeating Pompey at Pharsalus in 48, he campaigned in Asia (*veni, vidi, vici*), Africa and Spain. Since he was holding extensive offices such as *pontifex maximus*, consulship and, most importantly, the dictatorship which was only one step away from emperorship, Brutus, Cassius and others fearing for the survival of the republic assassinated him on the Ides of March (the 15th) 44 BC. His body, covered in stab wounds, fell to the base of Pompey's statue. Some of his writings survive, including the ever-popular *de bello Gallico* (Gallic Wars) and *de bello civili* (Civil Wars). From his name come Caesarean (his method of birth), Czar/Tsar and Kaiser and, through the town of Xerez, also known as Jerez, the drink sherry.

He has been played numerous times for TV, often adapted from Shakespeare, and in the cinema, most recently in the live action *Asterix* films and prolifically in a spate of sword and sandal Italian epics in the early sixties. Below is a cinematic selection:

Alain Delon: *Asterix at the Olympic Games* (2008)
Alain Chabat: *Asterix and Obelix: Mission Cleopatra* (2002)
Klaus Maria Brandauer: *Vercingetorix* (2001)
John Gottfried: *Asterix and Obelix contre Cesar* (1999)
John Gielgud: *Julius Caesar* (1970)
Kenneth Williams: *Carry On Cleo* (1964)

Alessandro Sperli: *Giants of Rome* (1964)
Ivo Garrani: *Son of Spartacus* (1963)
Rex Harrison: *Cleopatra* (1963)
Cameron Mitchell: *Caesar the Conqueror* (1962)
Gustavo Rojo: *Julius Caesar against the Pirates* (1962)
Gordon Scott: *A Queen for Caesar* (1962)
John Gavin: *Spartacus* (1960)
Reginald Sheffield: *The Story of Mankind* (1957)
Louis Calhern: *Julius Caesar* (1953)
Harold Tasker: *Julius Caesar* (1950)
Claude Rains: *Caesar and Cleopatra* (1945)
Warren William: *Cleopatra* (1934)

ROMAN AUTHORS

This is a short history of those authors worth remembering who have provided so many of the quotations in this book and inspired literature over the last two millennia.

Titus Macius **Plautus** wrote plays based on Greek

comedy, including *The Menaechmi* around 200 BC and provided Shakespeare with inspiration.

Quintus **Ennius** paved the way for Latin poetry despite little of his works surviving.

Publius Terentius Afer (**Terence**) was a former Carthaginian slave who wrote plays in the 160s BC.

Titus **Lucretius** wrote six books *de rerum naturae* in the first century BC.

Gaius Valerius **Catullus** was a poet flourishing in the 50s BC, famous for loving and losing Lesbia / Clodia.

Gaius Sallustius Crispus (**Sallust**) wrote the *bellum Catilinae* and *bellum Iugurthae*.

Marcus Terentius **Varro** was a contemporary of Caesar's, writing *res rustica* and on language.

Publilius Syrus, an actor of the 40s BC, is attributed with numerous maxims.

Gaius Julius **Caesar** received his own chapter (see p. CXIII).

Marcus Tullius **Cicero** (106–43 BC), known as Tully, was a politician and supreme orator, who came to prominence in 70 BC by prosecuting Verres, an unscrupulous governor of Sicily. In 63 BC he was elected consul and suppressed the Catiline conspiracy, executing Catiline without a trial. He was exiled for this in 58 but was recalled by Pompey in 57. As a staunch supporter of the republic and status quo, he regretted Pompey's defeat in the civil war (49/8),welcomed Caesar's assassination in 44 and proceeded to speak against Antony. When Antony allied himself to Octavian, he had Cicero executed. His head and right hand, symbolising his speeches and written words, were placed on the *rostrum* (speaker's platform built from the prows of ships) as a warning to others. He wrote prosecuting speeches (e.g. *in Verrem, in Catilinam*) and defending ones (*pro Marcello, pro Milone*), rhetorical works, philosophy and essays such as *de officiis, de amicitia* and *de senectute*. Because so many of his more informal and personal letters survive, Cicero remains one of the more accessible Romans, having a human condition which is recognisable as true then as today.

Publius Vergilius Maro (**Virgil**) wrote the *10 Bucolics* (*Eclogues*) of which number 4 generated much excitement for supposedly predicting the birth of either Christ or Augustus, the *Georgics* (4 books) and, the *pièce de résistance, Aeneid* (12 books).

Quintus Horatius Flaccus (**Horace**) fought with Brutus at Philippi. A biography by Suetonius documented his life. He wrote the *Epodes, Odes, Satires, Epistles* and *ars poetica*.

Titus Livius (**Livy**) wrote *ab urbe condita*, 142 books out of which 35 survive. Fan of Cicero.

Publius Ovidius Naso (**Ovid**) was famous for *Metamorphoses* and *Fasti*. Augustus exiled him to the Black Sea for writing naughty poems.

Phaedrus, author of fables, was a freedman of Augustus.

Lucius Annaeus Seneca (the Younger) left letters, Stoic philosophy and tragedies and was forced to commit suicide by Nero.

Gaius Plinius Secundus (**Pliny the Elder**) wrote *naturalis historia* and died at Stabiae after Vesuvius erupted.

Gaius Plinius Caecilius Secundus (**Pliny the Younger**), adopted by his uncle Pliny, wrote many letters, several to emperor Trajan.

Marcus Fabius Quintilianus (**Quintilian**) produced the *institutio oratoria* on rhetoric and was a big fan of Cicero.

Martial wrote epigrams in the reign of Domitian.

Plutarch wrote biographies on famous Greeks and Romans around 100 AD.

Publius Cornelius **Tacitus** was the son-in-law of Agricola, governor of Britain. He wrote the *Annals* and *Histories*.

A little bit of latin...

Any Latin, Will?

Ben Jonson said Shakespeare had 'small Latin and less Greek' in *Ode to Shakespeare*.

But *Love Labour's Lost* Act IV Scene 2 would appear to disagree. Holofernes, speaking to Sir Nathaniel and Dull, comes up with *sanguis, caelo, terra, haud credo, in via, facere, ostentare, bis coctus, omne bene, perge, pia mater, mehercule*, translating all the while and as Jaquenetta and Costard enter utters, *vir sapit qui pauca loquitur* – a wise man speaks little.

He then quotes Mantuan, '*Fauste, precor, gelida quando pecus omne sub umbra ruminat* – and so forth.'

This is from the 1st Eclogue of the late 15th-century poet Baptista Mantuanus which goes on '*antiquos paulum recitemus amores*' to mean 'Please let's reminisce over lost loves, Faustus, while the cattle chew the cud in the cool shade.'

Holofernes carries on with *lege domine, caret, imitari* and reprises with *pauca verba*.

Lord Say utters, '*bona terra, mala gens*' – nice land, rotten people – to which Jack Cade riposts with 'Away with him, he speaks Latin' in Henry VI, Act IV Scene 7.

Queen Katharine interrupts Cardinal Wolsey as he says, '*tanta est erga te mentis integritas, regina serenissima*' – there such a great integrity of mind towards you, o most serene queen – with 'O, good my Lord, no Lati,' in Henry VIII Act III Scene 1.

In *Measure For Measure* Act V Scene 1 Lucio tells Escalus *'cucullus non facit monachum'* – a cowl doesn't make a monk – talking about Friar Lodowick's integrity.

In Henry IV Act II Scene 5 Pistol's almost Esperanto-esque *'si fortune me tormente, sperato me contente'* – if fortune torments me, hope contents me – is not really Latin at all. But by Act V Scene 5 he manages *'tis semper idem for obsque hoc nihil est'*: while *obsque* is a bit obscure, it seems to mean 'It's always the same for without this there is nothing'. In the same scene Pistol reprises in a slightly different form *'si fortune me tormenta, spero contenta'*. He's making it up as he goes along, isn't he?

Shakespeare also used his knowledge of gerundives when it came to thinking up a name for Prospero's daughter in *The Tempest*. Thinking perhaps of *Amanda* (She who should be loved), he came up with *Miranda* (She who should be admired).

Decimus Iunius Iuvenalis (**Juvenal**) wrote 16 satires and spawned many quotable phrases like the Romans' sole interest of *panem et circenses*.

Suetonius was a biographer of Caesar and the first 11 emperors, writing during Hadrian's reign.

Marcus Aurelius wrote the Stoic *meditationes* while campaigning next to the Danube.

Ambrose was a 4th-century bishop of Milan with many religious writings.

Jerome translated from Greek into Latin the Vulgate Bible, completing it in 385 AD.

Claudian was a late 4th-century poet.

Aurelius Augustinus (**Augustine**) wrote prolifically, including *confessiones*.

PARTS OF SPEECH

Latin isn't all fun and games and egomaniacal emperors – when it comes to learning the language, one must understand the complexities that make it so compelling, but also so frustrating. There's going to be a lot of talk about parts of speech so here they are....

Parts of Speech	English examples	Latin examples
I. VERB	IS, LOVES	est, amat
II. NOUN	GIRL, BOY	puella, puer
III. PRONOUN	SHE, HIM	illa, illum
IV. ADJECTIVE	BEAUTIFUL, MY	pulcher, meus
V. ADVERB	IMMEDIATELY, NOW	statim, nunc
VI. PREPOSITION	TOWARDS, NEAR	ad, prope
VII. CONJUNCTION	AND, BUT	et, sed
VIII. INTERJECTION	GOSH!	ecce
IX. ARTICLE	A, THE	-

All words have to be at least one of the above and some particularly clever ones can be more than one depending on context.

English grammar is a minefield so to prevent your brains blowing up, here's a breakdown of those parts of speech, arguably simplified by a Latin perspective.

I. A VERB describes an action or state

Some are transitive, requiring an object, others intransitive, requiring only a subject.

It's so important, but these are the categories one will meet in Latin grammar.

a. **Conjugation** *1st, 2nd, 3rd, 4th, Mixed, Irregular*
b. **Person** *1st, 2nd, 3rd*
c. **Number** *Singular, Plural*
d. **Tense** *Present, Future Simple, Imperfect, Perfect, Future Perfect, Pluperfect*
e. **Mood** *Indicative, Subjunctive, Infinitive (Gerund), Imperative, Participle (Gerundive)*
f. **Voice** *Active, Passive (Deponent)*

English has retained most of the above but uses auxiliary words to come to the rescue.

II. A NOUN names a person or thing
See the separate section on cases.
a. **Declension** *1st, 2nd, 3rd, 4th, 5th*
b. **Case** *Nominative, Vocative, Accusative, Genitive, Dative, Ablative, Locative*
c. **Number** *Singular, Plural*
d. **Gender** *Masculine, Feminine, Neuter*

A noun formed from a verb is either a gerund or an infinitive.

A little bit of latin...

E.L. Wisty lives on

In the 60s revue, *Beyond the Fringe*, Peter Cook enjoyed a hilarious monologue as a monotone miner and failed judge, E.L Wisty, thus establishing Latin as rigorous, a tag which it has never really lost. Here is an excerpt from one of his many versions.

'... Yes I could have been a judge but I never had the Latin, never had the Latin for the judging. I never had it so I'd had it, as far as being a judge was concerned. I just never had sufficient of it to get through the rigorous judging exams. They're noted for their rigour. People came out staggering and saying 'What a rigorous exam,' and so I became a miner instead...'

English has done away with these categories apart from singular and plurals, which maintain some formidable exceptions (men cf. talismans, geese cf. mongooses, mice, oxen, stories) and imported many from other languages (criteria, seraphim, phenomena, fungi, oases).

III. A PRONOUN replaces a noun
a. **Declension** *very individual*
b. **Case** *same as nouns but no vocative*
c. **Number** *same as nouns*
d. **Gender** *same as nouns*
e. **Type** *Personal, Reflexive, Relative, Demonstrative, Intensive*

English has retained all the above to differing extents.

IV. An ADJECTIVE describes a noun
a. **Declension** *1st along with 2nd, 3rd*
b. **Case** *same as nouns*
c. **Number** *same as nouns*
d. **Gender** *same as nouns*
e. **Degree** *Positive, Comparative, Superlative*

An adjective formed from a verb is either a participle or a gerundive.

English adjectives are much simpler though there's the odd trap (blond; blonde) and they do enjoy degrees.

V. An ADVERB describes a verb
It enjoys the same degrees as an adjective, otherwise it's unchangeable.

VI. A PREPOSITION states the relationship between a noun or pronoun to something else in the sentence
It does not alter form.

In Latin it governs either the accusative or the ablative.

English prepositions change pronouns into the accusative.

VII. A CONJUNCTION joins together two nouns, phrase or sentences
It does not alter form.

VIII. An INTERJECTION is usually a single word used as an exclamation
It does not alter form.

IX. An ARTICLE introduces a noun, rather like an adjective, hence the preference of many grammars to number eight parts of speech

In Latin there is no definite or indefinite article but there is always the numeral adjective *unus* (one) if necessary. For all the various forms of verbs, nouns, pronouns and adjective, too numerous to tabulate in one sitting, you could do no better than consult the enduring and not always beloved bible of Latin grammar, Kennedy's *Latin Primer*.

A little bit of latin...

Quality advertising

A famous leisurewear firm decided that *mens sana in corpore sano* – a healthy mind in a healthy body – rather neatly embodied its philosophy, but its name couldn't be MSICS and so they researched another word for *mens* and came up with *anima*.

Another firm wanted to call its raincoat a shield against water: *aquascutum* fit the bill.

The entrepreneurial spirit of the Jameson family is represented on every bottle of Jameson Irish Whiskey, *sine metu* – without fear.

Harrods boasts *omnia omnibus ubique* – everything for everyone everywhere.

CASES

All Latin nouns are in one of seven cases. Adjectives have to follow suit with the nouns they agree with and pronouns use up to six cases.

Because there is no indefinite or definite article, such as German's *der, die, das* to indicate case (and number and gender), this can make life very difficult and Latin's several declensions make it worse. But there is little point in reciting noun declensions until the cases are understood.

English used to have cases but they have now been largely dropped and survive only in pronouns. (e.g. he, him, his; who, whom, whose; they, them, theirs) where they are called nominative/subjective, accusative / objective, genitive/possessive respectively. But this is good news.

Him was shot sounds wrong, preferring *He was shot*. So we have a nominative.

Me love she is rubbish whereas *I love her* does the trick. So *I* is nominative and *her* is accusative.

LATIN MATTERS

Case	Use	Example
NOMINATIVE	THE SUBJECT OF A SENTENCE	<u>Augustus</u> WAS SUCCEEDED BY TIBERIUS.
VOCATIVE	AN ADDRESSEE	'DO YOUR HOMEWORK, <u>boy</u>!'
ACCUSATIVE	DIRECT OBJECT AFTER CERTAIN PREPOSITIONS E.G. *ad, in, prope* TIME 'HOW LONG' PHRASE	I LOVE <u>cats</u>. THE WORM BURROWED <u>into</u> THE HAPLESS FELLOW'S BRAIN. HE RESTED <u>3 days</u>, I.E. <u>for 3 days</u>.
GENITIVE	POSSESSION 'OF'	<u>Caesar's</u> LEGIONS, I.E. THE LEGIONS <u>of</u> CAESAR
DATIVE	INDIRECT OBJECT 'TO'	I GAVE <u>to him</u> A TIP, I.E. I GAVE <u>him</u> A TIP.
ABLATIVE	AFTER CERTAIN PREPOSITIONS E.G. *a/ab, e/ex, in* TIME 'WHEN' PHRASE	THE ALIEN BURST <u>out of</u> THE TUMMY. THERE WAS A MESS <u>in</u> THE BODY. <u>by first light</u>, I.E. <u>at dawn</u>
LOCATIVE	LOCATES TIME, PLACE, STATE	<u>at/in Rome, at home, in the country, in the evening, at war</u>
NOMINATIVE	A COMPLEMENT APPOSITION (CAN BE USED FOR ANY CASE)	CICERO WAS MADE A <u>consul</u> IN 59 BC. THE EMPEROR, <u>Gaius</u>, WAS MURDERED.
ACCUSATIVE	PLACE WHITHER WITH THE NAMES OF TOWNS, SMALL ISLANDS, *DOMUS, HUMUS, RUS,* THE	HE RETURNED TO <u>Rome</u>.

CASES

Case	Use	Example
	PREPOSITIONS, *AD, IN* + ACC. ARE MERELY UNDERSTOOD IN LATIN. SPACE OF HEIGHT, DEPTH, WIDTH, LENGTH EXCLAMATION	HE DIVED <u>100 feet</u>. LUCKY <u>fellow</u>!
GENITIVE	POSSESSIVE AFTER GRATIA, CAUSA APPOSITION THE CITY OF ROME IS APPOSITION, BUT ROME WILL BE WHATEVER THE CASE OF CITY IS, AS THE PHRASE IS REALLY 'THE CITY, ROME BY NAME'	WITH THE GRACE <u>of God</u> THE ART OF <u>partying</u>
	ATTRIBUTION AUTHOR QUALITY VALUE (INDEFINITE) PARTITIVE SUBJECTIVE OBJECTIVE AFTER VERBS, *MEMINI, OBLIVISCOR*	LOADS <u>of money</u> <u>Virgil's</u> BOOKS, I.E. VIRGIL'S OUTPUT NOT HIS LIBRARY. THE RIVER <u>of 1 mile's length</u> was <u>of the deepest blue.</u> HE BOUGHT A TOGA <u>for a few denarii</u>. <u>2 of the ships</u> WERE LOST. THE REST SURVIVED. <u>Mother's</u> LOVE SAVED US. <u>Mother's</u> LOVE PROMPTED US TO SAVE HER. *I WAS MINDFUL <u>of our previous</u>* MEETING, I.E. I REMEMBERED.

LATIN MATTERS

Case	Use	Example
DATIVE	AFTER MANY VERBS, E.G. *CREDO, RESISTO*	I GIVE CREDENCE <u>to you</u>, I.E. I BELIEVE YOU.
	ADVANTAGE, DISADVANTAGE, REFERENCE	I DID THIS <u>for myself</u>.
	AGENT (ESP. AFTER GERUNDIVE)	THERE IS A DYING TO BE DONE <u>for you</u>, I.E. <u>You</u> MUST DIE.
	ETHIC (PERSONAL PRONOUNS)	<u>Mind you</u>, I KNEW WHAT I WAS DOING ONLY)
	POSSESSOR (TO STRESS POSSESSION)	THERE IS A HORSE <u>to me</u>, I.E. I'VE A HORSE.
	PREDICATIVE	IT HAD BEEN CONSIDERED <u>good</u> FOR ME.
	PURPOSE	REINFORCEMENTS WERE SENT <u>for helping</u>, I.E. <u>as a help</u>.
	DIRECTION (POETRY ONLY)	HE SWAM <u>towards the island</u>.
ABLATIVE	AGENT	BOND WAS ATTACKED <u>by the Soviet agent</u>
	INSTRUMENT	BOND WAS ATTACKED <u>with a knife</u>
	ABSOLUTE	<u>with Caesar leading</u>
	PLACE WHENCE	HE DEPARTED <u>from the house</u>
	SAME UNDERSTOOD PREPOSITIONS (*a/ab, in* + abl., *ex*) AS PLACE WHITHER RULE.	
	MANNER	<u>in silence, with great care</u>
	CAUSE	MOVED <u>by fear</u>
	SEPARATION	FREE <u>from debt</u>
	ORIGIN	BORN <u>from Zeus</u>, I.E. SON <u>of Zeus</u>
	COMPARISON	YOU'RE BRAINIER <u>from me</u>, I.E. <u>than I</u>.
	ASSOCIATION	FULL <u>with food</u>, I.E. FULL <u>of food</u>

Here are the commonest case uses:

The *ablative* has so many uses as it subsumed the *sociative*, also known as the *instrumental* case.

There are many other cases in other languages. Finnish, for example, enjoys the Partitive, Inessive, Elative, Translative, Instructive, Abessive, Comitative, Illative, Adessive, Allative, Essive and Exessive, mostly achieved by doing away with prepositions and having several variations of the Locative. *The Guinness Book of Records* attributes forty-eight cases to Tabassaran, a language of Daghestan.

GRAMMAR OF A VERB

A verb is a pretty essential part of speech as a whole sentence revolves around it. Unfortunately it attracts the most complicated grammar.

Here's one of those tables at the risk of provoking tears of nostalgia from some readers:

amo	I love / am loving
amass	you love / are loving, thou lovest
amat	he / she / it loves / is loving / loveth
amamus	we love / are loving
amatis	you love / are loving, ye love
amant	they love / are loving

OK, I've been slightly mischievous and put in a few archaic English forms but it does go to show that verb endings are a necessary evil as well as useful for appreciating Shakespeare.

But really, the most important verb, as in all languages, is *esse* (to be).

sum	I am
es	you are, thou art
est	he is, she is, it is, there is
sumus	we are
estis	you are
sunt	they are, there are

Amo is...

1st Person (hence the I rather than you or he)
Singular (I rather than we)
Present (happening now)
Indicative (fact)
Active (the subject is instigating the action of the verb)
1st Conjugation (it has a lot of 'a's)
and *sum* is the same except that its conjugation is irregular.

So a verb has a choice of;
Person *1st, 2nd, 3rd*
Number *Singular, Plural*
Tense *Present, Future Simple, Imperfect, Perfect, Future Perfect, Pluperfect*
Mood *Indicative, Subjunctive, Infinitive (Gerund), Imperative, Participle (Gerundive)*
Voice *Active, Passive (Deponent)*
Conjugation *1st, 2nd, 3rd, 4th, Mixed, Irregular*

Person and Number are just like English.

Tense is too but English has about twelve so Latin is simpler in that respect, though, it can be argued, that can mean loss of a certain precision. Here they are, for the English verb to send, but arranged as Latin would with adverbs to find the correct time scale, and only in the indicative (most common) mood.

Present
now I send / *am sending* / *am sent* / *am being sent*

Future Simple
soon I shall send / *shall be sending* / *shall be* sent

Imperfect
often in the past I was sending / *used to send* / *was being sent*

Perfect
once or twice in the past I sent / *have sent* / *did send* / *was sent* / *have been sent*

Future Perfect
by tomorrow I shall have sent / *shall have been sent*

Pluperfect
a long time ago I had sent / *had been* sent

Mood, and the term is used loosely to simplify things here, can cause the most upsets.

Indicative
is fact, I send / *I send* a letter

Subjunctive
is conjecture, I may send / *I may send* a letter

Infinitive
is a verbal noun, to send / *I want* to send a letter

Gerund
is a verbal noun, the sending / *the sending* of a letter is very important

Imperative

is used to give an order, send! *send* a letter!

Participle

is an adjectival noun, sending / I saw her *sending* a letter

Gerundive

is an adjectival noun, must be sent / The letter *must be sent*

	Person	Number	Tense	Voice	Case	Gender
INDICATIVE	1, 2, 3	BOTH	ALL SIX	BOTH	(NOM)	ONLY IF USING 4TH
SUBJUNCTIVE	1, 2, 3	BOTH	ALL EXCEPT FUTURE	BOTH	(NOM)	PRINCIPAL PART
INFINITIVE	-	-	PRES, FUT, PERF	BOTH	NOM, ACC	NEUTER
GERUND	-	-	-	ACT	ALL SIX	NEUTER
IMPERATIVE	2, 3	BOTH	PRES, FUT	BOTH		
PARTICIPLE	-	BOTH	PRES, FUT, PERF	BOTH	ALL SIX	ALL THREE
GERUNDIVE	-	-	-	PASS	ALL SIX	ALL THREE

What makes mood complicated is that they come in various persons, numbers, tenses et cetera, but below is a checklist of what is available for each mood, which may prove a useful *vade mecum*.

Voice
Active is when the subject instigates the verb's action; I love
  Passive is when the subject suffers the verb's action; I am loved.
    Deponent is a Latin-only voice where the verb has passive forms but translates as active.

Conjugation (i.e. the various forms in order)
Latin has four conjugations, traditionally *amo, moneo, rego* and *audio*, a mixed one and a few irregulars. A regular verb has about 140 endings.

  All verbs are supplied with its own principal parts, e.g. *amo, amare, amavi, amatum* or more spectacularly *tollo, tollere, sustuli, sublatum*: I raise.

  Conjugation matters for the first three tenses only. And the first two principal parts provide the stem so for the above example, they'll all start toll-.

  For the last three tenses, the 3rd principal part

provides the stem in the active, so sustul-, and the 4th principal part provides the stem in the Passive, so sublat-.

So now it's just a question of mastering the endings. Back to Kennedy's *Latin Primer*.

English has one conjugation, a few endings, and its own set of principal parts. Its most irregular is 'to be'. No surprises there. It's irregular in all languages, even Turkish where it's the only one.

On the other side of the coin, a Minnesotan Native American language has up to 6,000 verb forms. Various Inuit-Aleutian languages blur the difference between nouns and verbs with hundreds of inflections.

WORDS JUST BETTER OFF LEARNED

The first collection of words to master is the group of common prepositions, those which govern the accusative (*ad, ante, circum, contra, in, inter, per, post, prope, propter, super, trans*) and those governing the ablative (*a, ab, cum, de, e, ex, in* (again), *pro, sine, sub*). These all come with many English derivatives.

But the following words, a selection of the most common, are just better off learned as they are often hard to guess using derivatives and are especially useful when studying. But some do have certain logic to them so this list will be helpful.

Most are adverbs along with a few conjunctions.

LATIN	ENGLISH	USE
et	AND	NOT TO BE CONFUSED WITH THE VERB *sum*
-que	AND	ATTACHED TO THE END OF THE SECOND WORD
sed	BUT	-
tamen	HOWEVER / BUT	(THESE TWO ARE NEARLY AN ANAGRAM OF
autem	HOWEVER / BUT	EACH OTHE)
tandem	AT LAST / FINALLY	-
nam	FOR / BECAUSE	*nam* IS NOT A NEGATIVE
non	NOT	-
numquam	NEVER	-
iam	NOW / ALREADY	-
nunc	NOW	NOT TO BE CONFUSED WITH *hunc* (ACC. SING. MASC OF *hic haec hoc*)

LATIN MATTERS

LATIN	ENGLISH	USE
hic	HERE	A 'COUSIN' OF *hic haec hoc*, LITERALLY IN THIS PLACE
etiam	EVEN / ALSO	**et + iam**, AND NOW
igitur	AND SO / THEREFORE	-
magnopere	GREATLY	CF. THE ADJECTIVE *magnus*
bene	WELL	CF. THE ADJECTIVE *bonus*
saepe	OFTEN	-
inde / deinde	THEN / NEXT	-
solum	ONLY	-
iterum	AGAIN	ITERATE AND REITERATE ARE DERIVATIVES. CONNECTED TO *eo*
quoque	ALSO / TOO	LITERALLY 'AND WITH WHOM/WHICH' SO CONNECTED TO THE RELATIVE PRONOUN *qui quae quod*
cras	TOMORROW	-
heri	YESTERDAY	SURVIVES IN FRENCH HIER, ITALIAN IERI AS WELL AS IN HERITAGE
ibi	THERE	-
satis	ENOUGH	SATISFACTORY AND SATISFY ARE DERIVATIVES
sic	THUS	-
ita	IN SUCH A WAY / SO	
ita + que	THEREFORE / AND SO	**ita + -que**
mox	SOON	-
tum	THEN / AT THAT TIME	-
-ea adverbs		
interea	MEANWHILE	**inter + ea**, LITERALLY AMONG THINGS
postea	AFTERWARDS	**post + ea**, LITERALLY AFTER THINGS
-quam conjunctions		
postquam	AFTER	
antequam	BEFORE	

WORDS JUST BETTER OFF LEARNED

LATIN	ENGLISH	USE
quamquam	ALTHOUGH	
Originally ablatives		
hodie	TODAY	**hoc + die**, LITERALLY ON THIS DAY
frustra	IN VAIN	
forte	BY CHANCE	
subito	SUDDENLY	
lente	SLOWLY	
modo	ONLY	LITERALLY IN THE ONE WAY
-im adverbs		
olim	ONCE UPON A TIME	
statim	IMMEDIATELY	
-er adverbs		
libenter	WILLINGLY	
fortiter	BRAVELY	
nuper	RECENTLY	
celeriter	QUICKLY	
semper	ALWAYS	
brutes	-	
quam	THAN	
whom/which	IT ALL DEPENDS ON CONTEXT	
quod	WHICH	
	BECAUSE	AGAIN ON CONTEXT
si	IF	
ut	TO / IN ORDER THAT	
aut	OR	
doublets		
et ... et	BOTH ... AND	
aut ... aut	EITHER ... OR	
nec ... nec	NEITHER ... NOR	
neque ... neque	NEITHER ... NOR	

FURTHER SELECTED READING

S. R. H. James, *Latin I, Latin II, Latin III*, Able Publishing 1998 – 2007

Simon R. H. James, *London Film Location Guide*, Batsford 2007

F. M. Wheelock, *Wheelock's Latin*, HarperCollins 1994

R. Colebourn, *Latin Sentence and Idiom*, Bristol Classical Press 1987

B. H. Kennedy and J. Mountford, *Kennedy's Revised Latin Primer*, Longman 1994

S. A. Handford and M. Herberg, *Langenscheidt's Shorter Latin Dictionary*, Hodder and Stoughton 1966

British Hit Singles and Albums, Guinness 2005

Winston S. Churchill, *My Early Life: A Roving Commission*, Mandarin 1991

Nicholas Ostler, *Ad Infinitum A Biography of Latin*, HarperPress 2007

Harry Mount, *Amo, Amas, Amat… And All That*, Short Books 2007

Caroline Lawrence, *The Roman Mysteries series*, Orion

2001 – 2009

Conn Iggulden, *The Emperor series*, HarperCollins 2003 –2009

Robert Graves, *I Claudius* and *Claudius The God*, Penguin Classics 2006

Goscinny & Uderzo, *The Adventures of Asterix series*, Orion

J. K. Rowling, *The Harry Potter series*, Bloomsbury 1997 –2007

John Gray, *Lawyer's Latin*, Robert Hale 2002

John Gray, *Long Live Latin*, Canis Press 2004

Russell Ash, *The Top Ten of Everything 2007*, Hamlyn 2007

Lindsey Davis, *The Falco series*, Random House 1989 – 2007

Richard Fortey, *Dry Store Room No 1: The Secret Life of The Natural History Museum*, HarperPress 2008

Paul Sterry, *Complete British Wildlife*, HarperCollins 1997

The Internet

There are thousands of internet sites, begging for a Googling, starting with, for example;

www.roman-emperors.org
www.museumoflondon.org.uk
www.vam.ac.uk

Quiz Answers

QUIZ I: JAMES BOND FILMS (ANSWERS FROM PAGE XXVIII)

medicus minime: Doctor at the very least, i.e. *Dr No*
a sinistra civitate (cum) amore: From the left state with love, i.e. *From Russia With Love*
digitus auri: Finger of gold, i.e. *Goldfinger*

globus tonitrus: Ball of thunder, i.e. *Thunderball*
bis solum vivis:You Only Live Twice
regius locus in quo ludi pecuniae tenentur: Royal place in which games of money are being held, i.e. *Casino Royale*
in servitudine secreto pro regina (I.S.S.P.R.): In secret service on behalf of the queen, i.e. *On Her Majesty's Secret Service*
pretiosae lapides sunt aeternae: Precious stones are eternal, i.e. *Dimaonds Are Forever*
vivet et moriatur: Let him live and die, i.e. *Live And Let Die*
vir aureo telo: The Man With The Golden Gun
explorator qui me amabat: The Spy Who Loved Me
vir qui lunae imaginem removere conatur, i.e. is qui impossi bile somnium petit: The man, who tries to remove the image of the moon, i.e. he who seeks an impossible dream, i.e. *Moonraker*
tuis oculis solum: For Your Eyes Onl
animal cui sunt octo membra: Animal to which there are eight limbs, i.e. *Octopussy*
numquam dic numquam iterum: Never Say Never Again
consilium ad necandum/interficiendum: A View To A Kill

vivae luces diei: The Living Daylights
ei licet ut necet/occidat/interficiat: Licence To Kill
oculus aureus: GoldenEye
cras numquam morietur: Tomorrow Never Dies
orbis terrarum haud satis est: The World Is Not Enough
morere alio die: Die Another Day
regius locus in quo ludi pecuniae tenentur: Casino Royale
(again)
minima quantitas solacii: A very small quantity of solace, i.e. *Quantum Of Solace*

QUIZ II: NUMBER ONE HITS ANSWERS FROM PAGE LVIII

1953: *credo* (Frankie Laine; Robson & Jerome, 1995) 'I Believe'
1954: *tres denarii in fonte* (Frank Sinatra) 'Three Coins In the Fountain'
1955: *'liberatum e vinculis' carmen* (Jimmy Young; Righteous Brothers, 1990; Robson & Jerome, 1995; Gareth Gates, 2002) 'freed from chains' song, 'Unchained Melody'

1956: *est paene cras* (The Dreamweavers) 'It's Almost Tomorrow'

1957: *erit ille dies [in quo moriar]* (The Crickets) 'That'll Be The Day [That I Die]'

1958: *magni globi ignis* (Jerry Lee Lewis) 'Great Balls Of Fire'

1959: *quid vis?* (Adam Faith) 'What Do You Want?'

1960: *solum soli* (Roy Orbison) 'Only The Lonely'

1961: *ad me recta redi* (Everly Brothers) return to me directly, 'Walk Right Back'

1962: *terra mira* (The Shadows) 'Wonderful Land'

1963: *quomodo id efficis?* (Gerry and the Pacemakers) 'How Do You Do It?'

1964: *domus solis orientis* (The Animals) 'House Of The Rising Sun', *magnopere cepisti* (The Kinks) you've captured me greatly, 'You Really Got Me'

1965: *i nunc* (Moody Blues) 'Go Now', *mihi non satis est* (Rolling Stones) it's not enough for me, '(I Can't Get No) Satisfaction'

1966: *hae caligae factae sunt ad ambulandum* (Nancy Sinatra) 'These Boots Are Made For Walking', *viridianae herbae domi* (Tom Jones) 'Green Green Grass Of Home'

1967: *hoc est meum carmen* (Petula Clark) 'This Is My Song', *libera me* (Engelbert Humperdinck) 'Release Me', *silentium est aureum* (Tremeloes) Silence Is Golden'

1968: *quam orbem mirabilem* (Loius Armstrong; Eva Cassidy & Katie Melua, 2007) 'What A Wonderful World', *mihi tibi nuntiandum est* (Bee Gees) 'I've Gotta Get A Message To You', *parvo auxilio ab meis amicis* (Joe Cocker; Wet Wet Wet, 1988) 'With A Little Help From My Friends'

1969: *quo vadis, mea pulchra?* (Peter Sarstedt) 'Where Do You Go To My Lovely?'

1970: *omnia genera omnium* (Dana) 'All Kinds Of Everything', *anulus auri* (Freda Payne) 'Band Of Gold'

1971: *calidus amor* (T. Rex) 'Hot Love'

1972: *sine te* (Nilsson; Mariah Carey, 1994) 'Without You', *quomodo confirmari possum?* (David Cassidy) How Can I Be Sure?'

1973: *flava vitta antiquam quercum circumligate* (Dawn) 'Tie A Yellow Ribbon Round The Old Oak Tree'

1974: *illa* (Charles Aznavour) 'She', *quando iterum te vide bis?* (The Three Degrees) When Will I See You Again?'

1975: *si* (Telly Savalas) If, *navigo* (Rod Stewart) 'Sailing'

1976: *retine mihi omnia basia* (Brotherhood of Man) Save All Your Kisses For Me'

1977: *itaque iterum vincis* (Hot Chocolate) 'So You Win Again'

1978: *ter femina* (The Commodores) 'Three Times A Lady', *aetatis noctes* (John Travolta & Olivia Newton-John) 'Summer Nights'

1979: *clari oculi* (Art Garfunkel) Bright Eyes, *nuntius in amphora* (The Police) 'Message In A Bottle'

1980: *victor omnia vincit* (Abba) 'The Winner Takes It All'

1981: *mulier* (John Lennon) Woman, *nonne me cupis?* (Human League) 'Don't You Want Me?'

1983: *verus* (Spandau Ballet) 'True'

1984: *sciuntne diem natalem esse?* (Band Aid, also 1989, 2004) 'Do They Know It's Christmas?'

1985: *volo scire quid sit amor* (Foreigner) 'I Want To Know What Love Is', *move propius* (Phyllis Nelson) 'Move Closer'

1986: *noli relinquere me hoc modo* (Communards) 'Don't Leave Me This Way'

1987: *iterum vincis* (Bee Gees) 'You Win Again', *quis est illa puella?* (Madonna) 'Who's That Girl?'

1988: *is non gravis est, ille est meus frater* (Hollies) 'He Ain't Heavy He's My Brother', *tibi nihil debeo* (Bros) 'I Owe You Nothing', *perfectus* (Fairground Attraction) Perfect, *Olympus est locus, qui est in terra* (Belinda Carlisle) 'Heaven Is A Place On Earth'

1989: *aeterna flamma* (Bangles; Atomic Kitten, 2001) 'Eternal Flame'

1990: *nihil te assimulat* (Sinead O'Connor) 'Nothing Compares 2 U'

1991: *omnia quae facio, pro te ago* (Bryan Adams) '(Everything I Do) I Do It For You'

1992: *finis viae* (Boyz II Men) 'End Of The Road', *te sem per amabo* (Whitney Houston) 'I Will Always Love You'

1994: *ubique est amor* (Wet Wet Wet) 'Love Is All Around', *mane alium diem* (East 17) 'Say Another Day'

1995: *villa* (Blur) 'Country House'

1996:*noli respectare, irate* (Oasis) 'Don't Look Back In Anger', *tres leones* (Lightning Seeds, again in 1998) 'Three Lions', *vis esse* (Spice Girls) you want to be, Wannabe, *verba* (Boyzone) 'Words'

1997: *noli loqui* (No Doubt) 'Don't Speak', *candela in vento* (Elton John) 'Candle In The Wind', *numquam*

umquam (All Saints) 'Never Ever'

1998: *cors meum supererit* (Celine Dion) 'My Heart Will Go On'

1999: *volans sine alis* (Westlife) 'Flying Without Wings'

2000 *eheu!... iterum egi* (Britney Spears) 'Oops!... I Did It Again'

2002: *si cras numquam adveniat* (Ronan Keating) 'If Tomorrow Never Comes'

2003: *pulchra* (Christian Aguilera) 'Beautiful'

2004: *tibi faveo* (Girls Aloud) I give favour to you, 'I'll Stand By You'

2005: *adeone Amarillo?* (Tony Christie) am I going to Amarillo, 'Is This The Way To Amarillo', *es bella* (James Blunt) You're Beautiful, *me tollis* (Westlife) 'You Raise Me Up'

2006: *mihi ridendum est* (Lily Allen) I have to smile, Smile, *mihi saltare non placet* (Scissor Sisters) it's not please for me to dance, 'I Don't Feel Like Dancing'

2007: *quingenta milia passuum* (The Proclaimers) five hundred thousands of paces, '500 Miles'

QUIZ III: FILM HITS ANSWERS FROM PAGE LXII

Albus Niveus cum septem pumilionibus (1937): Snow White and the Seven Dwarfs

egressus vento (1939): Gone with the Wind

casa alba (1942): Casablanca

femina scelesta (1946 / 1980): The Wicked Lady

tertius vir (1949): The Third Man

caerulea lucerna (1950): The Blue Lamp

bellum mundorum (1953 / 2005): War of the Worlds

medicus adest (1954): Doctor In The House

et ego et rex (1956): The King and I

decem imperia (1956): The Ten Commandments

circum orbem terrarum octoginta diebus (1956 / 2004): Around the World in Eighty Days

dormiens pulchra puella (1959): The Sleeping Beauty

Maris undecim (1960 / 2001): Ocean's Eleven

superbi septem (1960): The Magnificent Seven

centum et uni canes (1961 / 1996): 101 Dalmatians

iuvenes (1961): The Young Ones

trecenti [Lacedaemonii] (1962 / 2006): The 300 Spartans / just called *300* in 2007

longissima dies (1962): *The Longest Day*
mea pulchra femina (1964): *My Fair Lady*
iuva! (1965): *Help!*
sonitus carminum (1965): *The Sound of Music*
ubi aquilae audent (1968):*Where Eagles Dare*
o, iecur! (1968): *Oliver, Oliver!*
proelium Britanniae (1969): *Battle of Britain*
fabula amoris (1970): *Love Story*
vir qui obtulit aliquid quod non recusandum erat (1972): the man who offered something which was not to be refused, *The Godfather*
sellae equitationis incandescentes (1974): incandescent seats of equitation, *Blazing Saddles*
turris ignis (1974):*The Towering Inferno*
dentes maris (1975): *Jaws*
bella stellarum : spes nova (1977): *Star Wars: a New Hope*
pons plus (1977): *A Bridge Too Far*
ea quae non nata est in terra (1979): she which has not been born on earth, *Alien*
imperium repugnat (1980): *The Empire Strikes Back*
currus ignis (1981): *Chariots of Fire*
id quod non natum est in terra (1982): it which has not been born on earth, *ET* (whose gender is never specified)

templum mortis (1984): *(Indiana Jones and the) Temple of Doom*

redite ad futurum (1985): *Back to the Future*

ex Africa (1985): *Out of Africa*

optima hasta (!) (1986): excellent spear, *Top Gun*

improba saltatio (1987): *Dirty Dancing*

ultimum iter pro bono (1989): ultimate journey on behalf of good, *(Indiana Jones and the) Last Crusade*

vir qui est similis mammali noctis (1989): man who is similar to a mammal of the night, *Batman*

umbra (1990): *Ghost*

domi solus (1990): *Home Alone*

femina pulchra (1990): *Pretty Woman*

silentium agnorum (1991): *Silence of the Lambs*

hortus antiquorum animalium (1993): garden of ancient animals, *Jurassic Park*

quattuor nuptiae funusque unum (1993): *Four Weddings and a Funeral*

leo regius (1994): royal lion, *The Lion King*

Romanus deus solis, tredecim (1995): Roman god of the sun 13, *Apollo 13*

maxima navis quae summersa est (1997): very great ship which sank, *Titanic viri in vestibus nigris* (1997): men in black clothes, *Men in Black*

tres viri infansque (1997): *Three Men and a Baby*

scriptor notus in amore (1998): famous writer in love, *Shakespeare in Love*

mater (!) (1999): mother, *The Mummy*

non in colle (!) (1999): not in the hill, *Notting Hill*

sextus sensus (1999): *The Sixth Sense*

illud quod subiacet (2000): *What Lies Beneath*

illa quae feminae cupiunt (2000): *What Women Want*

conveniamus parentes (2000): *Meet the Parents*

tempestas optima (2000): *The Perfect Storm*

cubiculum celatarum rerum (2002): room of hidden things, *(Harry Potter and the) Chamber of Secrets*

signa (2002): *Signs*

de puero (2002): *About a Boy*

heros araneus (2002): *Spider-man*

rex redit (2003): king returns, *(Lord of the Rings:) Return of the King*

inveniens 'no-one' (2003): *Finding Nemo*

amor re vera (2003): *Love Actually*

arca mortui (2006): *(Pirates of the Caribbean) Dead Man's Chest*

laeti pedes (2006): *Happy Feet*
ludi senioris carmina (2006): songs of the senior school,
High School Musical
expiatio (2007): *Atonement*
nulla patria senibus (2007): *No Country for Old Men*
erit sanguis (2007): *There Will Be Blood*

QUIZ IV: NUMBER ONE POP ARTISTS (FROM PAGE XCVIII) ANSWERS

1954 *porta est dies (!)*: door is day, Doris Day
1956 *textores somniorum*: weavers of dreams, The
Dreamweavers
1957 *cicadae*: The Crickets
1958 *semper pratum fratres*: always lea brothers, The
Everly Brothers
1961 *umbrae*: The Shadows
1963 *exquisitores* : The Searchers
1964 *animalia*: The Animals; *saxa volventia*: The Rolling
Stones
1965 *fratres iusti*: The Righteous Brothers, *petitores*: The
Seekers, *ilices aquifoliae*: The Hollies, *aves*: The Byrds,

apricus et divide (!): sunny and share, Sonny and Cher

1966 *fratres qui ambulant:* brothers who walk, The Walker Brothers, *vultus parvi:* The Small Faces, *pueri litoris:* boys of the beach, The Beach Boys

1967 *simii qui litteras ordinare non possunt;* simians who can't spell, The Monkees

1971 *aurora:* Dawn, *media via:* Middle of the Road, *necatus:* killed/slayed, Slade

1972 *novi petitores:* The New Seekers

1973 *decem vide vide (!):* ten see see, 10CC

1974 *limus:* Mud, *tres adiunctivae quantitates:* three adjectival quantities, The Three Degrees

1975 *regina:* Queen

1976 *hiems, ver, aestas, autumnus:* winter spring summer autumn, The Four Seasons, *res vera:* The Real Thing

1977 'lion' *orator:* Leo Sayer, *alae:* Wings

1979 *vicani incolae:* inhabitants of the village, Village People, *vigiles:* nightwatchmen, The Police

1981 *primus vir et formicae:* first man and ants, Adam and the Ants, *hominum foedus:* treaty/league of mankind, Human League

1983 *currisne? currisne? (!):* do you run? do you run?, Duran Duran, *tu, age quadraginta:* You act 40, UB40

1987 *stellarum navis:* ship of the stars, Starship

1988 *madidus, umidus, udus:* Wet Wet Wet, *tu quoque:* you too, U2

1989 *novi iuvenes in via:* new young men on the street, New Kids on the Block, *animi stulti:* Simple Minds

1990 *australis pulcher:* The Beautiful South

1992 *a pueris ad viros:* from boys to men, Boyz II Men

1993 *tene illud:* Take That

1994 *princeps:* Prince

1995 *arbores circum aquam in deserto:* trees around water in a desert, Oasis

1996 *puellae cibi acris:* girls of bitter food, Spice Girls

1998 *totaliter beatae:* totally blessed females, All Saints

1999 *gradus:* Steps, *Britannum genu, hastae:* British knee spears, Britney Spears

2002 *dulces infantes* or perhaps *mellis bellissimae:* sweet babies or perhaps very beautiful females of honey, The Sugababes